AF271768

# THE STORY OF MY LIFE

### As Told To Anita Bauer

### by Arnold Ehret

BENEDICT LUST PUBLICATIONS, New York, NY 10156

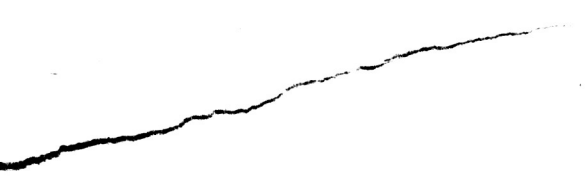

*BLP*———————————————

This *Beneficial* Book edition includes the complete text of Arnold
Ehret's autobiography as he told it to his secretary, Anita Bauer.
It is printed from brand new plates made from completely reset,
clear, easy-to-read type. Beneficial Books are published in pocket
book form by a division of Benedict Lust Publications P.O. Box 404,
New York, NY 10156

ISBN 0-87904-048-3

*Printed in the Unitd States of America*

# Contents

# Foreword

About two years ago Arnold Ehret came to me in a vision of the night, singing: "I have forgiven you. I now go to rest."

I knew then that he meant rest eternal and was strangely moved, for we had been friends and were so still, though a misunderstanding had parted us. However, I consoled myself with the thought that some day all would be explained and well, some day when I had finished writing the stories which he had told me and made him a present of them. As yet I read of his lectures in the papers and knew that he was still active.

Imagine then my sorrow when I learned that he was killed October 8, 1922! Too late now to explain. My dream had been true.

My second thought was: "Has he met Hilda, his beloved, in the great hereafter?" And then I remembered that once he had said: "Some day my biography shall be written." But little did I dream that this precious responsibility was to grace me.

I remember Mr. Ehret best as I saw him that first day, standing to receive me at the head of the stairs, tall, graceful, smiling, his soft brown hair brushed away from his forehead and curling in bobbed fashion about the back of his ears. He wore an Uncle Sam beard and untrained, unclipped mustache. His face was pale and slender, the blue eyes kind and singularly clear, the nose fine. I thought: "This is how a human being ought to look."

He held out a warm hand in welcome, led me into his room. Insistent tears blurred my eyes. I explained: "Please excuse this. I just had the news that one of my young brothers fell in the war."

To my surprise he didn't offer a word of consolation but stood as if he hadn't heard, arranging the pages of his manuscript. When finished he said gently: "Your address was given me at the business college on Kearney street.... You do translating, typing?"

We agreed about the work I came to do. He said he would call for it when finished. That was the whole of our meeting. Nevertheless, the world didn't seem quite as empty as before I came. All the way home Mr. Ehret's room came between me and the picture of my bereavement. I thought of his sensitive hands, the immaculate linen he wore and wondered how he made his living.

# 1

## My Silent Love

A few weeks later he brought to my house a small painting and set it upon the mantleshelf. Then, hands in pockets, as was his habit, he stepped back smiling his approval.

"It belongs here," he said. "Your place reminds me of it."

Looking, I saw a green meadow with a few trees in the background and a small, white shrine. White nuns were walking there to worship in the evening.

"The Isle of The Blessed?" I asked, having heard him speak of that. He shook his head.

"This is The Holy Grove. The other is a piece of land with the red glow of a sunset above." Vaguely: "There are many conceptions of blessed isles."

I begged: "Tell me about yours."

And, measuring the room with long strides, back and forth, hands in trouserpockets, head bent forward, he began his story.

"There was Hilda," he said, hesitant. "Many years have passed since this happened. Yet the picture remaĩns uppermost in my mind.... I am sitting, as it were, a bashful youth, in a place where she, a young waitress, is working. There is a certain battle of competition about the girl. She is a queen to whom I scarcely dare lift my eyes.... That delicate type which is subject to one of the world's greatest plagues and usually presents itself in a more spiritual beauty always has attracted me. It is the only kind that can.

"Hers are those clear, wonderful eyes, such as in contrast to other sick people are found in tubercular cases. Her slender body has the grace of something superhuman."

Interrupting himself he asserted: "Tuberculosis is, it seems, a force of nature aiming to bring about ideal conditions in place of all unattractive fullness of form due to overfeeding."

"But," he continued, "I do not detect any germ of the disease. Love and youth take health for granted. I simply sit there longing to approach without daring. And my bashfulness isn't the only barrier. There are the many students, her continual throng of guests.... Voluntarily I choose a table in the furthest corner, then tell myself that as amateur artist I have a keener appreciation of her charms and therefore a better right to worship than all those who court her." A dreamy smile. "There comes a day when my opportunity to draw nearer is waiting but her great beauty inspires me with such holy awe that I find no words.

"However, one evening—it is the last, before she goes away—my eyes met hers above the heads of students. And that penetrating look, that counterpart of evil, tells the mystery of a great love.... True love has no words.

"On the following day my queen has vanished. I search but find her no more. Soon after that also the restaurant is being closed. It has, in Hilda, lost its attraction."

After a silence he stated: That was chapter No. I."

"Yes," responded İ, eager to hear more.

# 2

# My Madonna in Munich

He said, stopping at the window, tugging at his beard: "It was my first glimpse of an isle of the blessed. . . . At that time I held a position as drawing teacher. Now I decided to serve the coming year in the army, choosing Munich as my garrison to study art during my hours of leisure.

"Visiting the many museums in that city two facts impressed me: that art, more than anything else is truth because it gives the privilege to present as natural and beautiful all that which to the conventional mind is sin. What astonished me as artist most, however, was the naive judgment of the learned laymen about art. There abounds a gap in all our education—.

"My deepest interest awoke Fritz Von Uhde, the great displayer of subjects from the New Testament. In his Sermon On The Mount and The Lord's Supper he transposed Christ into the present time. In all of his pictures he preaches the second coming of the master."

"He is light; from him proceeds light." quoted I, Munich and its art also being dear and familiar to me.

Mr. Ehret's eyes shone. We were like two happy children with our most beloved subject, religion, agreeing that Uhde has the Christian conception of the spiritual light of the world in his works, throwing a remark of surprise because of it.

"The cavalier, the captain of horses, that bony type of man, though slight in build," said Mr. Ehret. "Who would have thought it of him? Well, he caused enough displeasure and many a shake of the head at first. But no painting of the old masters has the illumination that proceeds from his Christ. He has made his belief in spiritual light so artistically real. . . . I myself believe that Christ was not only the light of the world in a spiritual sense but that his body actually shone. All forms do if their owners live the true life. The halo around the head of saints is not a thing of imagination. It's a fact."

"Ah," said I, "if one knew how."

"Know how!" replied Mr. Ehret bitterly. "Who cares to know? The average person is satisfied with

himself—too satisfied! That is the trouble. Why,
when I returned to take up my old position as teacher
at the higher technical school in Frankfurt I felt like
Nietzsche among my friends. Hungry I sat at their
table, hungry and exhausted!"

He spat the words out but smiled again the next
minute, his mind back in Munich. "There is a little
bakery on Turken street," he was saying, "made
important by a charming little maiden.... As every
volunteer has to purvey himself with provisions, it
also happened that I had to buy myself a piece of
bread now and then. And, of course, I always went to
where the little madonna face smiled at me from
behind the counter—a face quite exceptional in type
and beauty. Now, every time I came to the store to buy
five Pfennig's worth of bread the piece was wrapped
up with greater care and grew larger. And finally I
went there even without the need of bread, just to see
a work of art, for she always reminded me of a
painting by some old master.

"An officer of the same regiment also admired her, as
I learned one day when lingering in the back of the
store in civilian clothes, while he was stalking back
and forth by the window. He grew aware of me, and
the idea that one of his subordinates should get the
better of him vexed the man. Two months later I
happened to come under his command and was the
first to be punished for bad step.... A miserable
revenge!"

"But the girl," I wanted to know, anxiously, "what
became of her?"

He resumed his walk and made no reply. Presently he said: "The interesting fact in my artistic career is that only certain types attracted me.... When after about ten years I came back to Munich my first walk was through Turken street to see if at least the bakery was still there.... It remained. But owner, help, all had vanished. Where may they be, those beings?"

"What seldom happens, I was called back to my old position, there where formerly Hilda had been."

# 3

# Early Meatless and Drug- less Influences

At another occasion Mr. Ehret told: "Of my whole life I have the impression that I was an exception among my friends. Circumstances threw me to the learned, and there, as said before, I felt like Nietzsche, hungry for truth and seriousness and knowledge, yet always experiencing the disappointment that the conversation was about some piquant love-affair or politics. In gloomy half-consciousness I roamed through the world.

"Having studied in Frankfurt, I had been longing to return there. Any young person would; there is something warm, unifying about college life, like the feeling for home.... And my old companions received me with loud rejoicings.

"However, this show of respect and feeling of triumph quickly passed. For I had resolved not to be drawn any more into their circle of intellectual stagnation, but to use all of my power to accomplish the highest in my work. That they resented.

"About an hour's distance from me lived my mother. I felt best when visiting her and talking to the old peasants, guessing that in their seeming ignorance was great wisdom of life. My whole aim was always for simplicity and nature.

"One old fellow in particular seemed wiser to me than my twenty-four colleagues. Frank was his name, and he was one of the tallest men in the village, a giant; the people therefore called him the Turk. His house was the last on the village street with a wide look over the vineyards, fields and gardens.

"And not alone was he the largest among the peasants but also the shrewdest and wisest, the original type of a healthy and altogether natural being. Tall, the slightly curved nose of the philosopher, he always walked with bowed head, giving the impression of a terribly serious being. Yet in conversation he was the greatest wit. Even in misfortune he could put the right wit in the right place.

"This authority of so called national wisdom and wit had peculiar sayings about which, as a child, I greatly pondered. 'If the mallet hits you,' he would say, 'you may be sure that its handle will hit you too!' And I would gaze at him admiringly and resolve: 'I shall be like Frank when I am grown. Yes, I shall be exactly like he.'

"He was the only friend of my father's household, and if some day he didn't come we were alarmed and thought he must be sick. If late, father or sister looked anxiously at the clock, asking: 'Why is not Frank here as yet?' And mother predicted that he is one of those few exceptions who die without warning.... He was our whole world.

"Even before I was able to talk correctly, at the early age of three, he played a greater role in my life than father or mother. On long winter evenings, when Frank was sure to call regularly, the entire household was in expectation an hour before time. And then the gate opened and fell back in its trap, the little one by the window whose expectation had been keenest, exclaimed with loud joy: 'Now comes the appletree!' With that the retiring day threw a radiance over the family, especially over the child's face.

"I called Frank the appletree because he always had an apple for me in his pocket.

"He was the only one among farmers, who, beside agriculture, appreciated a good fruit tree, and consequently had the best tented orchard. He differed from them by not bringing his fine fruits to the market Saturdays and taking home sausage and tid-bits.

"'Why should one carry the best to the rich people in the city?' he said. 'The junk they manufacture there is anyhow good for nothing. And," chuckled Mr.

Ehret, "he boasted of going there but once or twice a year, to the city that was only an hour's distance away."

The main theme of his narration wound itself chiefly around the time of his hard work and experience as a carter before trains were in existence, especially from the Rhine into Wales during the French wars. And what this born philosopher emphasized most thereby was the voluptuousness, the luxury of culture, which he denoted as evil. In that he was a Rousseau. And a thousand times he projected the triumph over a wanton life in making known that he ate his first piece of meat at his confirmation and the second at his wedding.... It was his veto against luxury to have reached the age of twenty-six before tasting the second piece.

"At that time there was only one butcher in the village, and when the second opened his slaughter house he said: 'One should not wish that man any luck, else the people will begin to eat meat even on work days.'

"If indeed he should arise today," reflected Mr. Ehret drearily, "there are four butcher shops in the place."

I placed before him a clipping wherein one of our ablest newspaper writers advocated the eating of flesh for brain work. Having read he replied with a humorous twinkle: "We justify ourself by our acts. That man probably is as fond of steak as another of alcohol or any such artificial stimulant, and so tries to make a virtue of his weakness.... Frank did splendid and strenuous work without all this. And so

have millions of others. Moses showed his people the
way back to health and the promised land on a
bloodless diet.

"The most wonderful thing about my old friend was
his memory. It was fabulous! Not only could he recall
beyond a half-century how the weather had been
each year, if the vintage was good, or the harvest
destroyed by hail, but he also gave accurate information about each individual month. And that this
wasn't imagination could be proven inasmuch as his
narrations of a thousand times always conformed
with each other.

"He preached against railroads, the public house and
card playing. And," smiled Mr. Ehret, "the modern
hats of maidens were not at all to his liking. 'If I was a
young man once more,' he said, 'I wouldn't marry
such a scarecrow!'

"To city life and society he was opposed not only by
instinct, but mainly because of experiences as
servant to a rich lady whose son studied medicine
and who, with his companions, often came to
celebrate. But the wine grown in those years must
have tasted good to the students, for Frank often had
to bring them to bed, and usually laid them on straw
in the barn.

"One of them tried to kill Frank, in his intoxication.
Later he became a physician. And when for the first
time in his life Frank needed a doctor, having
wounded himself with an axe, he went to this Dr.
Werder.

"'And,' asked he, 'who are you?'

"'Well,' said Frank, 'don't you know? I once upon a time took the knife from the student's hand and brought him to bed. I am Frank—you court counselor or whatever you may be!'

"The doctor says: 'That has to be cut open.'

"'Good,' says Frank, 'have you a sharp knife?'

"'Now look aside that you don't get sick,' advised the doctor.

"'Go to,' replies Frank. 'Can't I look to see if you are doing it right?' And he watches. The wound was bound up. Having related in the twilight of our sitting room his experiences of the day, he concluded: 'I would only like to know what kind of a bill he is going to make out for this.'

"At the appointed time he again went to the doctor. And he, greatly surprised about the unusual quick healing of the wound, said: 'No pus! No fever! Look, Frank. What a good thing that I gave you that medicine. As quick a healing as this is otherwise impossible. I shall, for safety, prescribe you another dose. Have you already used all of the first?'

"Frank answered: 'I haven't used any medicine at all. Do you think I use such devilish stuff of which I do not know what it is?'"

How Mr. Ehret enjoyed himself telling those little tales! He was still a boy and Frank was walking the road of life before him. I asked: 'You attribute the quick healing to his simple way of living?'

"Yes," he said. "Frank was eighty-eight years old and read his newspaper still without glasses. Furthermore, there was not a tooth missing in his mouth. When referring to his age someone asked if he hadn't any fear of dying, his drastic answer was: 'More calves are led to the slaughter house than oxen.' Confirming in a brutal manner the fact that when a being has passed a certain age, he has, in his simple way of living, less to fear than others. Fewer people die between the age of fifty and eighty than at any other time."

Looking at Mr. Ehret with his bowed head, listening now to his wit, now to his sharp critic, I thought how well he had succeeded in making himself into the likeness of his old friend.

# 4

# My Father

"I was brought up with the religious belief: pray and
be good," Mr. Ehret said during one of our walks over
the heights of the city. "This belief followed me
through my college years. In Karlsruhe, where
during our extensive trips to nature we always loved
to discuss the subject religion, I fell out with one of my
friends because of his unbelief. Later I myself
reached the point where the beautiful women in
church interested me more than the preacher. I
became indifferent to religion.

"At the higher school one does his work well enough
to pass a fair examination and otherwise the whole
sphere of interest is pleasure women. In time I lost (as
the world presents it) even the last spark of faith. And
with my religious belief also went my superstition.

"The whole of my parental habitation and that of my grand-parents was, in no small circumference of the country, surrounded by the light of mysticism. My grandfather had the reputation of a sorcerer. He was veterinary surgeon but healed both man and animals with sympathy and a few simple remedies of nature.

"I once painted his portrait and hung it up in my room, and when one day a stranger happened to see it he exclaimed: 'By thunder! This fellow resembles the old William I.'

"My grandfather was a born aristocrat and wore precisely the same beard as the beloved old emperor. And, like he, also ate always, up to the last, never more than a bowl of milk and bread for supper.

"His remedies, which he used in all cases, plant, animal and human, the casting out of devils of the possessed, etc., were hereditary. And so was his reputation. It fell upon my father of whom all kinds of mysterious and adventurous tales were told. The saying that he did not fear the devil himself and had laid low seven devils one time was proverbial with the villagers.

"As a child this caused me much annoyance and suffering. The children at school would tease me about it. But later, as far as I was concerned, this superstition itself went to the devil.

"My father was one of the most singular beings in existence. He was a farmer but practised on the life of man and animals as successfully as grandfather. There isn't a sphere of human knowledge in which he was not active. Even his enemies had to admit, that, while making no pretense to be more than a simple farmer, he was a genius as a technologist.

"One finds dilettants in all departments. Of father it was told that as an eighteen year old boy he constructed by an oil lamp in their barn a pocket knife with twenty-four blades, not inferior to the work of the finest mechanics who have the advantage of every machine.

"In our house were instruments of all sorts of handicraft: a little smithy, a masonry, a small joinery, etc. Father made all of our farming tools and even repaired his own watch. A wine-cask he made that caused the admiration of every professional workman.

"When in later years sickness chained me to the bed I thought about all this and read a book dealing with occultism, spiritualism, etc. And then I found things as scientifically investigated facts, such as were told about my father but which at that time I had thrown overboard as superstition.

"Today I see it all in a new light.... I began to investigate deeper, put an advertisement in the paper for some one interested in spiritualism. Meetings were held. My state of health grew worse. I searched for truth; went to another city, and was disappointed in everything, especially in the spiritualists.

"I began to investigate alone and learned to know an author of special branch, Dr. Du Prel of Munich. He photographed spirits and weighed them.

Following these communications, Mr. Ehret and I often sat in the dark in my bare front room, laying hands on a little table. Before long it began to move, and he repeated the alphabet until some name or message was spelled. I eagerly expected to hear from Hilda or his father but they didn't come. Somehow, I had taken their being beyond the grave for granted, and later was told that they were.

# 5

# The Holy Grove and a Love Child

Mr. Ehret had spoken about how, as a child in the country, he had longed to see the big cities.

"But," he said, "I soon lost all interest in them, and with resignation to comfort, looked about for an abode in the suburbs."

He chuckled: "I came to a policeman's house, who, having committed some blunder, was sent to prison for several weeks and his wife exerted herself to spread the tale that he had gone to some place of pilgrimage. Then," he continued, "I found a home with a gardener.

"He had a small house but the most beautiful flower, fruit and vegetable garden. In summer it was The Holy Grove.

"There were two original types in that little house, built after the chalet style of Switzerland. The ground floor was somewhat elevated and a slope of flowers ran up to the windows, so that without difficulty one could walk in through that. When Frank came to see me he said: 'This is convenient for forbidden calls.'

"Nearby flowed a little brook. Everything breathed peace and contentment, the garden and its owner. And that in the midst of the millionaire district of the city. Often the gardener could have sold out for a goodly sum but preferred to live as a poor man in a beautiful garden to being rich in a closed mansion.

"Dear old Sebastion! As a young man he had lived long in foreign countries, had a fluency of languages and a large viewpoint, but remarked always that there was nothing above his garden and that he loved it more than all the world. His main products were flowers, especially roses, and there didn't pass an hour of the day without one of his customers (the rich ladies of the vicinity) calling to buy and converse intimately with him, calling him Sebastian.

"I, the young stranger, often wished that people could be as confidential with me. I didn't know that this confidence was a deserved jewel bestowed by nature only upon the sympathetic and meek.

"About fifty years of age, slender, with a slight stoop, Sebastian always had a cigar stump in his mouth, which, however, never was lit. His voice was high-pitched like a young girl's, and he was very religious. His favorite dishes were sweet corn and baked apples with syrup.

"Sebastian's household was taken care of by Sabine, a distant relative of his, a type of strictly religious piety. She was even more pious than Sebastian. It shone out from her face. But, back of that visage, still charming in old age, lived a sorrow, a disappointment, and a very large secret, as I discovered later.

"Notwithstanding all simplicity everything in that household breathed a consecration, every small utensil and cooking vessel. A happiness and peace was there such as isn't found even in the happiest wedlock. About her young guest, Sabine was as deeply concerned as about Sebastian.

"But the secret—he read it!

"There should be certain evenings in a home when each could tell of another's shortcomings without giving offence. It should be holy truth. I often thought that little Sabine could have been spared lots of suffering thereby.

"She read only in prayer books and was without friends. But many a time I longed to be near her again, in that clean, orderly kitchen, where on Sundays she always served a roast beef—the best I ever tasted.

"The secret which I believed to be reading in her face caused her sleepless nights even then. She could tell every morning—with motherly right—what time I came home.

"'At one twenty,' admitted the young student.

"'Correct,' replied Sabine. And Sebastian with his girlish voice remarked: 'Yes—thus the young people will have it. They like to sit at the tavern.'

"Often, too, I went through the window so as not to disturb Sabine.

"Now, the relatives of Sebastian were anxious that he should sell the garden and retire, obvious with the intention that some day the inheritance could be taken possession of in ready cash. 'But' reasoned Sebastian, 'to whom shall I go? They all want me—Fritz, Jacob, Karl. I shall however not depart from my home. I shall leave a firm will.'

"Had things remained with the little house and garden all would be well, instead of the process that followed later.

"Sabine, too, was rich and it was said that she carried her wealth in her stockings. Her heirs, who were partly the same as Sebastian's, worried more about her future disposal of property than his. . . . One heard whisperings of some secret. And when one day my sister informed me about it I understood their anxiety, and also why Sabine had to pray so much.

"Sister, who didn't expect any inheritance, but was otherwise intimate with Sabine's family circle, confided in me with the greatest discretion.

"'Sabine has a son,' she said, and made me promise not to show or tell that I knew anything about it. 'He is professor of theology in Tuebingen, the same as his father was in whose house Sabine, as a girl, had been cook.'

"Sister, who at that time was an orthodox church woman herself, regarded this as a scandalous offence. My thoughts, however, were quite different, particularly since I now knew who that ideal being was, that handsome, intelligent youth whose picture graced Sabine's writing desk. This, then, was her son! A child of love. I began to see light.

"Just imagine what must have quaked through this little soul, Sabine, when I asked her at times who this beautiful being was! 'He looks like an ideal of a clergyman,' I said. 'A magnificent being! Who is he?'

"'Oh—he simply is a young clergyman like others,' replied she.

"'No!' I affirmed. 'He is better than others. He is of all the only one who forcibly impresses me.'

"Later I heard her happy voice, singing in the kitchen." A frown took the place of Mr. Ehret's contemplative smile, as he continued: "I taught fifteen years at a higher technical school where there were usually from ten to fifteen hundred pupils, and where in conferences and registry one has an accurate account of things. There it was shown that among scholars the illegitimate children were the most intelligent."

Talking as if to himself, he said: "I am viewing my lowest class—children from nine to ten years of age. And, as has always been the case with me, I pay more attention to a person's appearance than to anything else. If only I see the hand of a pupil I can make out his report in drawing. His name I never know.

"Among the fifty little fellows there is one who particularly holds my interest. I ask him: 'What is your name, and who is your father?'

"No answer. I ask him again, say harshly: 'Can't you tell me who your father is?' Then the beautiful child sighs: 'I have no father as yet. My mother is cook at the Chapter.'

"The sigh of this child was an impeachment against the whole world!" Mr. Ehret cried. "It shocked me more than all the doctrines of philosophy put together!

"When taking up duty at the school the gray, aged principal told me: 'All of your predecessors were terrible. They could keep no discipline. The last one was poor in health and the children often tyrannized him.'

"But," he reflected, "the guilt always falls back on him who deserved it. The highest art of a teacher is to be just. I later heard from impartial sides that the children feared me most but also loved me best.

"As mentioned before, my memory of the ear was bad. Among my thousand pupils I never knew how one of them was called. But the better was my

memory of the eye. It went so far that, when seeing
the face of a pupil in the street, I also saw his drawing
with every one of its faults and could have just as well
given him a correction there and then.

"For abstract things my memory was good only in
extreme cases, in a good and bad sense of the word.
There was once a character who among all of my
colleagues was justly considered a criminal type.
Once this boy dared to lie to his drawing teacher. It
vexed and worried me much. But, to exercise justice, I
did not let him feel it. Later I told him why, and also
his reason for misusing my justice. I said: "'I shall
never forget you this.'

"After many years, when meeting him in the street,
he still showed his fear of me, evidently remembering
what I told him."

I asked Mr. Ehret if he ever met little Sabine's son, if
he hadn't ever come to see his mother. He was
surprised to think that I should expect it. "How could
he," he said. "Nobody was supposed to know of his
existence. His father raised him from childhood up.
Besides, granted that our laws are wrong—they
nearly always are when dealing with affairs of the
heart—the fact remains that the illegitimate child
can hardly be expected to thank its mother for its
inheritance of shame."

"My own mother told me a narrative that, when
many bad spirits were present, it stank so that one
could hardly endure it." Mr. Ehret said once. "When
two soul organs belong together they smell one
another. 'Never shalt thou ask,' says Wagner's

Lohengrin. Or, if my nearness, my quiet being does not tell that I am yours I do not belong to you. Two souls belong together throughout eternity; they must feel each other on earth and strive to perfect themselves until they are gods."

I thought he was thinking of Hilda and himself. But presently he spoke again of Sebastian's garden.

"It was not only in the daytime so exceptionally beautiful," he said, but especially in the evening. Then it had something quiet, mysterious, for it lay in a remote quarter of the city where the street lanterns did not disturb it. One only heard the babbling of the little brook.

"Not far from it was a large park and in it lived a nightingale. To hear its song people came from far and near. It's music was better than any concert.

"Late one day I came home across the country. My Uncle's house was by the lake where in June there are so many glow-worms that everything gleams. The nightingales sang their duet. The moon threw a faint light. I was enraptured and, gathering a little pile of hay, lay down there to rest.... Ay, you sweet rest in the arms of nature! My bed at home was not half so good.

# 6

## My Beloved Appears Again

"It was very late when I finally started to go. The street lanterns were turned down. Sebastian's garden was so dark that one couldn't see anything at all. Suddenly I run against someone, am scared, believe to have fallen into the hands of an assaulter, but see only how a form rushes by, so slightly, so quickly, so fragrant, that I have to consider if it really was a human being or a spirit. I went to bed with somewhat alarmed feelings.... In the vicinity of this garden lived a certain retired general.

"He and I passed one another for several years, feeling that some day we should learn to know each other. Our meeting was somewhat cooler than usual when he was in company of his wife, who was a good customer of the gardener and bought many and beautiful roses from him.

"To me this woman was of peculiar interest. It seemed that I had known her some time in the past, even though it may only have been in a dream. I never had a chance to see her closely. But as often as the general and she visited Sebastian's garden there was, evidently on both sides, the feeling that something connected us and would some day bring us together. Likewise there was a certain timidity, an undefined anxiety, something uncertain which the moment of our acquaintance would bring to light.

Both of us knew that there was danger. And when they were in the garden and plucked flowers, and I happened to be going or coming, I always took the side path to avoid meeting them.

"With such feelings I tried to influence Sebastian to learn more about this couple.... It became known that the general was an eccentric fellow, that he owned a large estate on the Russian border where before his marriage he had tasted life to the full, so that now his state of health was such that he had to withdraw himself from the whole of his own society. Yes, it even was whispered that contrary to his former extravagant way of living, he went to the opposite extreme, drank no more alcohol, used no tobacco, and ate no more meat.

"At first everyone believed that the couple led an ideal married life because they found it unnecessary to spend their time in company of others. In no theatre or place of amusement they were to be seen.

Presently the curiosity of neighbors was aroused and, as customary, all kinds of rumors were heard about this childless pair. The strangest tale was that he, an officer of high nobility, had married a much inferior woman, not only a commoner, but from the lowest class. Evil tongues even asserted that some time, somewhere, she had been a waitress and a disrespectable person. This, they said, was the cause of the officer's discharge from the army.

"However, as often as I saw this woman, I had, beside the constant recollection of having known her before, an impression which in no-wise corresponded with the rumor. On the contrary, there was something aristocratic about her.

"Five years later destiny commanded me to take better care of my health, and by chance the general and I got acquainted. It happened in a health resort by the lake in Geneva of Switzerland.

"At first a cool reserve was shown on both sides, the cause of which I attributed to the distance of social position. And besides, I too was now known to be a singular person. Nevertheless, little by little our reciprocal interest grew, especially since he asked every guest's opinion about his manner of proceeding with an ideal hygienic way of living. He was nothing short of pedantic in the care of his health.

"His wife was a pale, in comparison to him, truly aristocratic being. Especially when she talked one was convinced of noble blue blood on her part more than on his. And when she smiled—which seldom happened—a charm went out from her face that could gladden even the most sorrowful being. But as soon as that cheer-bringing smile was gone one received the impression that she was not a happy woman.

"The sanitarium was more modern and advanced than others. One didn't spend one's time mainly with food and drink. Much care was given to physical exercises; gymnastics, work in the garden, mountain climbing, etc.

"On the summit of the mount was a small house belonging to the sanitarium, and when one received orders to climb up there it always meant going without the mid-day meal. Only soured milk and bread was served after the long walk, but that tasted good. The little place itself was a wonder of simplicity.

"One day I happened to meet the general and madam there, and learned that they were going away next day. Now, she had a very large hat and could not get it into her box, and since I was provided with a good sized trunk I offered to take care of it. The couple were going to take another large trip through Switzerland.

"When they came back I fulfilled the special wish to personally deliver the hat. This wish had been expressed with an invitation to supper.

"The excitement! I was invited to Hilda's house! For it was she. I had known it right along, but we didn't dare tell each other.

"This was the first time when the tension between her husband and myself was somewhat loosened.

Not that he was jealous. The strain simply was due to the secret which only two of the three of us knew—perhaps—for there was no opportunity to ask if the other apprehended. No sign. Only painful uncertainty on my part whether she had committed herself to him about our former acquaintance, and that I knew who she was.

"He told me with certain impressiveness the Christian name of his wife. 'It is Clara,' he said. And he called her Clara only.

"When at a fitting opportunity I asked him, he told me that at one time she had used another name, but really was christened Clara, and he emphasized thereby that she was of good Italian race. I restrained my desire to ask why she had used another name.

"A large dwelling for three people," said Mr. Ehret offhandedly. "Superfluous rooms, partly endowed with old style furniture, stuffed with tableware and articles of luxury which all may have had their definition for the former worldling and his family, but at present served no purpose.

"With ironical pride the general opened a special buffet and showed me a rare collection of the most various kinds of champagne glasses, remembrances of so-called good times, which were, as he now acknowledged, the cause of his downfall. In this point particularly he had turned to the other extreme and had no respect for a person who indulged in his once so beloved alcohol.

"Having conversed about a few things, memories of the sanitarium, etc., the third and last being in the

large house came into consideration: the servant girl.
Madam introduced me to her with the remark that
she is a true, good soul who splendidly managed the
household since the first day of her married life. That
the girl was all that one could see in her face, and
besides, she wore a little golden cross around her
neck.

"The master of the house then informed me with
great confidence that we were to have a selected
hygienic meal and that his wife herself had helped
with it.... There were, to my conception, very good
things, but too many. And when at the end a variety
of imported cheese was served of which the lady said
she was very fond, I was inclined to believe her
husband's story that she was Italian.

"Generally people draw near each other and often
become intimate when sitting opposite at the table. It
was so with me. In that short time I learned more
about the couple than during all the previous years of
our acquaintance.

"The general had a very red and deformed nose, and
when alluding to it I asked if that was due to his
former way of living, he emphatically denied it and
said that not alcohol but a fall from a sleigh was the
cause. But the greater pains he took to convince me of
the fact the more I read in the eyes of his wife a deep
horror. Stood I here before a strange riddle?

"This former waitress who always gave me the
impression that her soul was of great nobility, had
been, through suffering, lifted still higher. To her
husband's coarseness she expressed no aversion. Her

countenance even remained unaltered when with a condescending smile he said: 'Just think! My wife and hired girl are so pious that they go to confession together.'

"Although I myself took the Catholic religion, as understood and manifested at present, the genuine piety of Hilda inspired me with new respect.

"She could not be recognized at once and was no longer as beautiful as formerly. Her face was puffy. She had grown stouter. However, she had known me at first sight.

"Two or three years pass over that evening. I come regular and often to the house. Yet Hilda and I are never alone. Finally an opportunity of about five minutes offers itself in the kitchen, and there is an animose love scene in which Hilda tells me she lives in hell, and if it weren't for the good girl, Lina, who is one in faith with her, she would have made an end by going into the water long ago.

# 7

## An Unhappy Marriage

"I remember a romance by Zola. When reading it I told myself: 'That could never be.' Now I must live to see that it is even worse than Zola describes it.

During those years, whenever I visited his house, the general had tried to appear as an ideal being. He always spoke excitedly about the possible good of mankind, denouncing its vices. Hilda he called his angel—which she was. And now she told me that he treated her like the devil.

"The astonishingly artful hypocrisy of the man! Performed with a direct routine. When once we were alone he expounded to me concerning what might be done with money. Now I knew. In those five minutes a whole life had passed before my eyes.

"Hilda told me that only through despair she had become waitress that time. But the heavy work had been too much for her and ruined her health. This unhappy marriage gave her back her former social position. She was of noble family.

"Her husband's ill-shaped nose was the result of a crime he had committed during the first part of their married life. That also had cost him his position as an officer. She herself had suffered much through self-reproach and developed chronic headaches. He took a position in Africa, where the heat made things worse. And when her mother advised her to abstain from meat, she threatened her with corporal punishment if she wouldn't help to consume the eternal leg of mutton.

"She had been seeking relief from some ailment other than her headaches about which her husband said it was something suspicious. One day she went with her mother to a doctor a specialist in sexual diseases. He told her that she was incurable.

"That was all of the embrace in the kitchen. Yet Hilda trembled with fear of sin. She would have to confess it next day in church.... The confessor admonished her with edifying words and made her promise to banish all thoughts of the beloved one from her mind. As punishment she was ordered to say five rosaries daily. When later he asked her if this had been efficient she said no, that thereby it grew worse. He told her then that in the name of God she may think about him, but if it would come to a divorce she would surely have to go to hell.

"I myself felt unspeakably sorry. I saw an eventual tragedy coming, acted apparently cooler, and began to avoid the house.

# 8

# Almost a Clergyman

"A few months later I am sitting one evening in a cafe in my home town, where those first experiences with Hilda took place. Vis a vis are two students who evidently talk about me. They look continually in my direction. Suddenly one of them, whom in the meanwhile I have recognized as a former pupil of mine, arises and comes toward me. He summons me to testify to his companion that I am their former teacher.

"The two of them had made a bet—one recognizing me, the other saying that it was impossible. Only when hearing my voice was he convinced. He gave vent to his astonishment with the remark: 'There is no trace of resemblance with the former drawing

teacher left in you. Only your voice convinces me. I
have lost my bet.'

"I replied: 'You are correct, even literally; the
drawing teacher of old lies in his grave. This is a new
being standing before you'.... And it was so."

There are few churches in San Francisco that we
didn't visit, but hardly ever during service. Both of us
preferred their silence, of which Mr. Ehret said that it
spoke loud enough.

"Even though one doesn't believe in a certain creed,"
he remarked, "one cannot help feeling the prayers of
the thousands of souls that come here."

Then he related how narrowly he escaped becoming a
clergyman.

"I never had any desire to study, but my father had
set his heart upon it," he said. "My two older sisters
as well as my mother naturally were for theology.
They themselves were ardent church members who
would not have missed service on Sunday for the
world. I, however, resisted the idea with all of my
energy. Finally I submitted to their urge and entered
the school of technical science.

"We were in the field one day, during my vacation,
and sisters and I disputed about the old subject.
'There, now, he costs money,' they said, 'but will not
become a preacher.'

"'The devil!' replied I. 'If it has to be I shall become
one, but a Lutheran.'

"One of them then became furious and shouted, lifting a beet: 'Tell me why! Or I shall throw this at your head.'

"'Because,' answered I, 'the Lutherans are permitted to marry.'"

Mr. Ehret chuckled. He was now about forty-five years of age and still enjoyed single blessedness. "The irony of fate!"

Then: "A few years passed by and my father died. I could have taken his place on the farm, together with my older brother who was sickly, but was no longer fitted for it. Perhaps I never had been.

"When coming to the city I was the oldest and last in my class at school, and had to take an examination before being admitted. At home in the village our old teacher often came into the room and marked a certain lesson to be copied, then went opposite to the tavern. Consequently my ignorance, and why the technical school only took me on trial.

"One of the teachers there, the instructor in French, resembled an international rogue more than an educator. His special aim was to hold up my country ignorance before others, so that I always went to school with beating heart.

"Later I heard that he cheated people and that no woman was safe in his presence. But at any rate, when after two weeks he had made our sample work he came and whispered in my ear: ''Tis well. You will not be dismissed from school.'

"According to his prophecy we were promoted, I from the last place to the third."

# 9

# A Broken Engagement

"Previous to that second meeting with Hilda I became ill," Mr. Ehret had said and proceeded to tell that, before the appearance of that illness he experienced a betrothal.

He smiled: "After it had been broken I went to a friend in the Black Forest, where together we pursued art.... He later told all of my friends about it." Then seriously: "The affair became deeply tragic for me, for the girl was the daughter of one of my colleagues with whom I naturally was thrown together at various occasions and collegiate festivities.

"She had awakened my interest not through any special or remarkable beauty, as was the case with Hilda, but to my artistic eye there was something

about her which the European maidens in general
didn't possess. She was unusually slender and neat,
with a mobility and manner that reminded of
Oriental blood. The artistic temperament. Her song
and skill at the piano were far above that of average
talented daughters.

"I believe it was that song from her charming mouth
which caused my entanglement. For though I didn't
particularly care for her nose, there was something so
beautifully sensitive about that mouth that I had
only one longing: a kiss from those rosebud lips."

With knitted brows he reflected: "The whole impression was that in reality she had no beauty.

"When for the first time I was invited to her house she
was in the kitchen and came to receive me in a large
apron. To my sorrow I had to discover later that this
kitchen apron had been calculated to give the
impression of domestic industry, even at the cost of
etiquette at such a first, conspicuous call. I saw
through the excuse when she told me she had been
helping mother, but also noticed that this simple
apron increased her charm." He threw an amused
glance. "Her aim to please had been accomplished in
another way. I liked her far better thus than in
society or ball dress.

"If only all girls would leave off their costly
garments and appear in simple clothing! I often
wondered why one sees so many beautiful faces in the
Salvation Army, and then I happened to think about
the hat, which in its simplicity forms such a
wonderful background.

"The girl's mother was a corpulent woman with a rather inexpressive face. She had the habit of putting on her golden eye-glasses at every occasion, even if unnecessary. One noticed plainly that thereby she aimed to give herself a more intelligent appearance. Another peculiarity was that she talked very little, always in an undertone, and that in conversation she agreed with everybody, whatever the argument.

"One would take her to be the most peace loving person in the world. Yet in all of her movements, in all that she said, was something precautious, painstaking, no matter how composed she acted. It was abnormal.

"That I, a psychologist, shouldn't discover what it was. Later, when forced to see it, I tapped myself on the head for not having suspected it before. She always was drunk, and I believed this to be her natural disposition!

"Still, the family was highly respected and moved in the best society. . . . On the outside splendor; behind closed doors the reverse. One night the mother and her two daughters were at a ball and returned home late, towards morning. I called at their house at four in the afternoon. There the old lady sits at the table, beside a bottle of beer and both of her daughters' new dresses. She said: 'See how industrious I am. I have changed every bit of trimming on those dresses since last night and cooked the noon meal besides. I haven't slept a minute.'

"'But,' said I, astonished, 'what for?'

"'Well,' replied she, 'don't you want to go to the theater tonight? And you know, when one moves in fashionable society one has to look like something—new ribbons—new things—'

"That, to me, was a blow on the head, and immediately the idea of an excuse came. I told her that I could not go to the theater that night. She said that the two girls were still asleep and explained, regarding the dresses: 'This gives the impression that they are wearing entirely new garments.'

"I felt myself growing another degree cooler."

Mr. Ehret had joined in my interrupting laughter. But suddenly his brows again met in disapproval.

"Such a degenerate subject!" he exclaimed disgustedly. "She would have made an excellent mother-in-law!

"'You know,' she confided, 'if one houses strangers one has a good deal of worry and has to use all kinds of tricks. I have duplicate keys made for every room, and when the people are out I go in and look after things.'

"One of my friends, rooming there, had become suspicious about this, and every Sunday when he went away he invited a friend to stay there. He would have caught her had she come in.

"There is, among wooers, the well known proverb: If you want to take a damsel look first at her mother; is she of good habits then you may ask for her daughter.

"I began to discover in my fiancée more and more the vices of her mother, and thus the final catastrophe prepared itself. First I had a parting of ways with the father because of falsehood, and when I met my former beloved again she admitted that all was true, but threatened to kill me unless I married her. Of course, that left me cool. A threat, made audible, is harmless.

"I packed up that day and went to the Black Forest, to my friend. There then we sat in the evening at the tavern, at peace, celebrating the end of my betrothal. Suddenly the door is jerked open; my friend's sister appears asking us to hurry home. Two excited ladies are there, wanting me, she said. I suspected at once who they were, and really found them to be my would-be mother-in-law and her daughter. They had learned my whereabouts through my sister and didn't hesitate, but took the next train to induce me to come back. This, of course, I couldn't. But to avoid a scene I told them to go to bed, that tomorrow we will talk about it.

"The following morning my friend and I were gone. We had taken a mountain trip, climbing overnight, and if my head had been heavy then, when we reached the summit I was as sober as a cat.... My former fiancé and her mother took themselves home again.

"This mountain climb was my salvation. My mind became free. My feelings reached out, onward. That day-break up there was the happiest in my life. My wrong step had been blotted out.

"Once I met a friend who had betrothed himself the same way as I, a nice, kind, industrious business man, who had just then taken possession of his father's place. He said to me: 'I have heard that you have brought about a conflict with your prospective mother-in-law. How can one do such a thing? Mine isn't any better, but—well, one has to stick to one's promise.'

"He went into this trap and a few years later he was insane."

# 10

# Ehret Grows Sick

Mr. Ehret had danced in my bare front room in the twilight, sung and whistled and then partaken of the scant supper in the kitchen where a newspaper took the place of a tablecloth, salt and pepper were served in jelly glasses, and a chair minus its back, and a soap box were our seats. Good old times, those! I, a young enthusiast; he a celebrity. There was just enough tea in the house to make two cups. And I had invited him only because he stayed late, thinking that he would decline, as usual. But he accepted, and worse. By mistake he put salt into his tea, and I had no other to offer. So he drank it like a hero. It sobered his mood, however, for the dancing and singing of the day was over.

"I grew sick," he related later, in the dark. "A five years' path of suffering began. Taking a long leave of absence from school, I went to all of the different watering places, but without result. Finally I had to give up my position altogether.

"'Nourishing food,' said the doctors. And I followed their instructions until one day I no longer could walk. I had become so weak. I frequented the best restaurants, where one dined excellently. Among those present was an American lady. As happens in such cases, every well-meaning person has new advice to give, and she sat beside me and saw how wretchedly ill I was and how I counted my pulse, and heard what others told me to do.

"Once she said to me: 'Don't count your pulse, and do not believe that so young a man has to go to ruin. I shall bring you something tomorrow.'

"She was the most sensible of all. The next day she brought me a prospectus of a Kneipp sanitarium in southern Alsace.

"When I think with what feelings I went to that place! I knew that its proprietor was a Catholic priest, and I was more anxious to see him than the sanitarium. During the whole night of my departure my imagination made pictures of the man who was to save my life. A tall, slender, elderly priest my phantasy saw him to be, who with Christian love cares for his patients.

"I received a sad disappointment. Precisely the same commonplace type of a Catholic clergymen as Kneipp himself! A thick head and a large belly.

"But there was an ultimate, patriotic life at the institution. Notwithstanding all misery, I still had a large share of my old humor, and soon new jokes made their round through the place. Even the honored clergymen, who were present in large numbers and as a matter of fact always occupied the best quarters, became interested in this strange newcomer of the second-class. I made peculiar acquaintances.

"There were old, typical Alsatians, staunch men, who loved to talk about war and the like, but also wanted to know this and that about their condition. And since the priest was to be seen only twice a week, it didn't take long until they brought their questions to me. Finally they came with all about which they disputed in tedious hours.

"A nice young priest made certain attempts to convert me. Although I was so beloved that, when leaving the place, most of the people were in tears, and though my opinions were valued so high that even the proprietor asked my advice on many occasions, there lay a serious shadow on me: I was the heretic of the whole institution avoiding the daily mass at the chapel.

"That young priest and I had many an interesting conversation about it. He wasn't a religious fanatic. 'Don't you pray?' he asked.

"I replied: 'No. I too have a God, like you. Only I am unable to picture His sudden interest in a being, and besides abolish a law of nature, since for years that being didn't bother itself about Him.'

"There had been a visible improvement in my condition, when all at once my old terrible kidney pains returned and I had to go to bed. Priest and doctor stood helpless at my side. The situation was critical. Nothing could any longer inspire me with the will to live; nobody could console me—until the nurse came.

"She was a beautiful French woman in the dark attire of a nun. She couldn't speak any German and my French wasn't very good. But whenever she came to visit me I felt better... A charming child!

"She said: 'The priest takes a special interest in you. Only one thing is missing. You have never been seen at the chapel.'

"I noticed how gladly she came. Besides her official calls she often spent an hour with me in the evening, always letting me feel that she was trying to convert my soul. But it was more than that.

"One night she wouldn't leave until I had promised her to go to the chapel, when well enough, and this promise I was permitted to seal with a kiss of her hand.

"Barriers!" Mr. Ehret sighed. "The holy vow! I made no attempt to break it, of course. But oh, how I should have loved to!.... One fine morning she brought me the first rosebud from the garden."

"And, I asked, wanting to hear more. He had lapsed into silence. "You felt better?"

"I wept!" he replied. "I had wept only twice in my life, and the third time was now when the pain nearly drove me insane and future prospects were despairing... A few days later I left for the watering-place Wildingen, going half way into the domain of medicine."

He sputtered: "'Tis a fraud, the whole thing! One drinks the water and pays terrible bills. If there had been an improvement there was no trace of it left when after some time I returned home. There I dragged myself through the winter. In February I experienced a radical change.

# 11

## Two Apples a Day

"Have you ever loved a place on earth so that you wanted to take it into your arms?" he asked. "Lichtenthal by Baden-Baden is a place like that. There I lived through the first months of my resurrection romance. It was the most beautiful time in my life.

"My belief in medicine was gone entirely and now I took my first step into another world whose existence one hardly suspects. A new period began.

"Lichtenthal is one of the most beautiful little places I have ever seen. It stretches itself towards the Black Forest. In the midst of the valley a small mountain is

pushed from which one has a wonderful view. There a
being of nature dwells, the greatest enemy of
medicine, a mad-man.

"I had previously inquired about him in Baden-
Baden and was told: 'Yes, he lives out there in
Lichtenthal, this strange fellow who gives his
patients nothing but two apples a day and a glass of
water, and besides has them run about naked.'

"There then I went with great expectations, as
excited as when going to the Kneipp institution. And
when the man stood opposite me a thrill of pleasure
went through my being. What a different impression
from the preacher in Corpoch at the French border!
There that obese, fat priest, here a Tolstoy, an ideal,
just as impious and free as every medicine apostate.
About sixty years of age, the same clothing, carriage
and appearance as the great Russian, and he also
wrote many books. Formerly he had been a baritone
singer in Cassel.

"That original consultation! I told my people about it
later.... I came to him, complained about my pains,
and he said: 'What? Pains? That is your own fault.
There was no pain in paradise, but neither were there
any chops. Eat fruit instead of sausages and such
nastiness, and throw off your rags and take air-
baths!

"That was the whole interview! He had but one
bath-tub at the place and that was rusted. There
were, however, plenty of shower-baths. The house
was one story high with projecting veranda, and the
whole front was only one room deep, so that every

room had a porch on the south and an entrance from the north, all built of wood, rather primitive.

"The main thing was the garden. The rooms were supposed to serve only as sleeping chambers. Even in rainy weather he chased his patients outside. He himself was, as he asserted and also showed, 'terribly weather-proof.'

"There was work to be done, sawing wood, digging, shoveling, garden work. Also a bowling alley was there.

"He held the most rational opinion regarding nutrition. I loved to hear him talk about it. Though not an orator, he presented everything so clearly and drastic as the former actor was wont to do. Often he came over to dinner from the small house close by, and producing two beautiful apples from his pocket, said: 'Look, you! In one of those apples is more nourishment and health than in the whole dinner.'

"When I came the institution did not really belong to him any more; he had sold it to a teacher from Magdeburg. But the teacher was not to be compared with our Tolstoy, who moved away. Thus it happened after a few weeks, since the new proprietor was unable to give his patients satisfactory explanation, that they always said: 'Go and ask Ehret.'

"As has been the case in Alsace, all kinds of interesting individuals were present: privy counsellors, actors, etc., but one tune and one harmony. People, who otherwise never thought of associating, were brought together through suffering. There was, for instance, a baron, about thirty-five or so, fat, stupid as those worldlings usually are, and he actually received only two apples and a few figs per day. The feelings that thereby arose! People used to high life—I too have experienced it.

"There also was an actress from Brussels. She had paralyzed fingers. If she wanted to pick black-berries in the garden she bent down and bit the berries off.

"I teased: 'If now your admirers should see you they would be shocked!'

"She answered appropriate and short: 'I would gladly give my whole fame and splendor and admirers for my health!'

"This exalting contrast to the other, the priest's institution. It was for me a secure road upward, to health, and likewise changed my whole conception of life. There gradually came the insight of what Gruebel calls: 'The worthlessness and even harm of culture.'

"The idea interested me more and more and I decided to look closely through those new spectacles of truth. Three months later I went to Berlin."

I mocked lightly: "To enjoy culture to the full."

"No!" he retorted. "To learn of anything new in that direction.... There was much—many interesting people.

"One remarkable fellow, a Catholic priest, and as it happened, a countryman of mine, had been crowded out of church because he talked too much about liberty. Looking for another livelihood, he would take anything that offered itself at the university: medicine, philosophy, etc. An original being. He introduced me into the scientific life of Berlin.

"At the different lectures there was always something new, contradictory being taught, and we went every evening. There were anarchistic meetings, and all of the reform movements; anti-medicine, socialism, physical culture, the Salvation Army, etc.

"On Sunday mornings, instead of going to churches as of old, we went to free religious lectures. One organization always gave a magnificent concert: song and wonderful organ play. But the philosophy of natural healing and vegetarianism attracted me most."

He sighed, chuckled: "Of all the disappointments! I went through Gruebel's school. Large pots, pans and spoons were brought. They stuffed, gulped.

"Ground reformers"—he reflected. "That society accomplished wonders. In the neighborhood of Berlin there was a sandy desert and they transformed it into a little paradise. It is called by the right name Eden. This colony is co-operative. As soon as one member passes away his share of possession goes back to the society—the only society worthy and able to exist.

"I also went to the university in Berlin and heard and saw all kinds of things, which, when viewed by light, tended only to lead people astray—let alone benefitting them.

"Among the many professors there was but one who forciby impressed me, and, strangely enough, he too lectured about the unusual theme: The harmful influences of culture upon the life of man.

"He represented a new, free Christianity, and of all the speakers he had the largest audience.... His antipode of the descendence theory of Darwin also had many hearers. But, although I had little or no religious feelings left, I always went to the former. His was an interesting looking theologian head, whereas the other's stupid face always reminded me of the waiter in our lodging.

"They defended two opposing ideals: the one God, Christianity; the other the contrary. Both were instructors.... When one reflects about those young students, how much was stuffed into their receptive heads, all the useless, characterless teaching. It has to go to pieces in time."

# 12

## Spiritualism/ Immortality

"Once I gave lessons in drawing at a high-class boarding school," he said at random. "To teach at such a feminine place had always been my longing. But in all my life I experienced no sadder disappointment. The life of impudence and ill-breeding in pupils I never had seen. One of the teachers didn't hear well and they played all kinds of mischief with him.

"There was one fine girl of great beauty. Her hair had the scent of roses. I asked what she was going to study. She said: 'Medicine.' That perplexed me. How could such an exquisite, womanly creature desire to uproot the intestines of dead beings in order to find the truth of life? Five years later she was by chance introduced to me as Fräulein Dr.——. A character type. She had not aged, but every bit of soft, feminine charm and comeliness and innocence had disappeared. She looked learned. I could never again have fallen in love with her."

One of our favorite themes was the investigation of spiritual movements. Mr. Ehret had seen so much of it. It had been part of his study in Berlin, where there is plenty of opportunity—about twenty spiritualistic societies are there.

"I had read many books about the secret world," he said, "attended many lectures and meetings. But I received the impression that, as with most things, speeches are being made but nothing positive comes to one's sight or hearing.

"At that time there were two renowned mediums in Berlin. One, the so-called flower medium, A. Rhode; the other had the strange name Abend. (Evening.) From that Rhode it was asserted that the spirits brought her flowers. However, my belief, which had already been shaken by visiting different societies, received another shock. She was convicted of fraud.

"Her meetings were held at a friend's house, an astrologer's. In that large, long-stretched room four or five gas flames were burning, making the place as light as day. I sat at the upper end when she entered, a witch-like, lean person. She gave me the impression that she was gifted with supernatural qualities.

"One heard sounds of rapping—which could have been true. But what seemed suspicious to me from the first was that there sat at her right and left two of the stoutest women, nearly covering her.

"Now, the impressionist, through a good speech learned by heart, had averted all attention from the medium, and in the next moment flowers were seen falling from the ceiling. There was general surprise. When, however, he again began his speech, I did not look at him but at the medium, and as the second flower came down from the alleged spirit world I plainly saw its source.

"That was half a year before the bluff became known and she was unmasked. When searched it was found that she wore a false petticoat full of flowers. From that she took one after another and skillfully threw it back of her to the ceiling and, of course, the flower had to come down from above.

"The swindling in itself provoked me less than this boundless vulgarity under the name of divine benevolence, which the speaker always emphasized.

"I had my doubts about the second medium, too, of whom it was said that she had still greater ability. She was a so-called materialization medium, and one could not get admittance as easily as by Rhode, who charged five marks fee. One had to be introduced. The director of the association, however, promised to make me acquainted with her husband, supposed to be a poor shoemaker.

"I met him, and at the same time a certain doctor. Now it seemed strange that Abend said to the doctor and me that he didn't know when the next meeting would be, to give him our address. Then, when the doctor wasn't looking, he whispered in my ear: 'Come Tuesday. I don't want the doctor.' That made me suspicious. But on the respective evening I went to the meeting.

"It was in a better part of the city. Evidently the poor shoemaker had, through the spiritual eye of his wife, acquired considerable property.

"I was introduced to many titled people, in particular to several members of the house Von Moltke. It even was whispered that the Kaiser was there, masked.

"One corner of the room was partitioned off by a curtain that parted in the middle. Every visitor had the right to invesitage this closely, also the garments of the medium to be worn in the meeting. They lay upon a chair. To convince that there was nothing hidden she undressed before the whole audience. Then she entered the cabinet, the curtains were closed and the room darkened.

"The spirit began to speak. It was a mixture of pietistic phrases and prophetic allusions, to me empty and meaningless. Then all at once he commanded: 'Darken entirely!' All of the lights were put out, so that one couldn't see a thing, the curtain parted about two feet wide and one saw a white figure soar twice past the opening. I suspected that the medium was swathed in silk-mull.... As a rule the spirit took time to transform itself.

"The medium mentioned the name of some loved one beyond the grave to an elderly couple. At all events, she had made correct inquiries. Tears ran down the old man's cheeks. Later the shoemaker knelt down and thanked God for having again shown grace to his wife.

"Many of those present undoubtedly believed the swindle, for although the police sought her some time after this and she made her escape, their faith in that sort of thing had not been swept away.

"I myself was still concerned about the various questions of life and salvation, the many currents of the spiritual sphere, theosophy, etc., but left disappointed.... That was Berlin.

"About the family Von Moltke it is known that they are spiritualists, and for that reason strained circumstances arose between them and the imperial house. One evening several masked gentlemen of the royal family took part in the meeting, and one of them—as was whispered—was the emperor.

"To me this tendency to spiritualism was explainable in as far as the genial old strategist, Moltke, was deeply religious. He wrote a book about his favorite book, the Bible, which reads like Christian Science. One would hardly expect it from a winner of battles. What staggered me was that the aristocracy of a country, which at the same time should represent spiritual nobility, could fall for the deceptive plotting of a shoemaker's wife.... Well, one pockets the thing and lets it go at that."

# 13

# A Child in my Image

"I had a strange dream," I said one day to Mr. Ehret.

"Ah?" he replied, interested. "I can explain dreams. Yes, I can."

So I told him that it was about Hilda and himself and a little fisher village. "Then, to my amazement, I realized that it wasn't Hilda who stood beside you but I," I concluded.

Mr. Ehret laid a hand across his eyes, and for a little while said nothing. He didn't always answer at once, so I waited. And what I heard had been worth waiting for. He told queer, simple, little, awkward me that he and I were kindred souls. My heart swelled with pride.

He nodded seriously: "I have known it from the first. And we shall meet again in the hereafter." Then: "The little fisher village—Hilda—It's Askona! She was there with me."

"Oh," responded I eagerly. "She was?"

"Not in the flesh, though," he said. "We never met again on this plane. But she wrote to me. And that is almost too terrible to relate. She would rather be horsewhipped for half an hour to being embraced by her husband, she wrote, yet she continued to live with him for fear of eternal condemnation.... We escaped from the conflict with a clear consciousness.

"But I will tell what women often overlook: Hilda expected a baby and wrote that during the time of her pregnancy, when her husband kissed her, she closed her eyes and tried to imagine that it was I. Later I went with the photograph of her child to a lawyer and he told me that, if the husband accused me of adultery, he would have to testify at court that I am the father. The child was such an image of me.

"Yet for two years and more Hilda and I hadn't seen each other. We were parted by a whole country. She wrote me her experience during that time, that her husband was greatly pleased about the expectation of an offspring. When, however, he perceived the remarkable resemblance between the baby and his wife's former friend, and she too had to acknowledge the same, he accused her of infidelity.

"One good thing was that he knew Hilda and I were never alone together and the possibility of actual adultery was out of question. Nevertheless, since he could not discover any trace of his fatherhood in the little one, he made life so miserable for her that she died.

"Partly to blame, of course, was the fact that she was inclined to consumption. Under those circumstances it is possible that a woman may give life to a healthy offspring but she herself is ruined.

"After his wife's death the general joined religious movements and played a certain big role in life by giving large sums to charitable foundations. He became one of those so-called benefactors of humanity.

# 14

# Discovers the Value of Fasting

"I never had answered any of Hilda's letters. I couldn't, and she did not expect it. So utter darkness prevails about much. I didn't even know of her death until she came in spirit to Askona.

"In the meanwhile much had happened to me. Having returned from Berlin I found that the question of immortality pursued me more than ever. I put an advertisement in the paper and thereby came into a so-called private circle, where the meeting began at a table.

"Here nobody was the medium, but one of my friends brought his three unmarried sisters-in-law and that spoiled the freedom. One always tried to make a match between them and some present young man, one of whom was my former pupil who later played a big part in my life by taking a trip on wheels with me around half of the world.

"He and I finally agreed to separate from the crowd, together with another man whose name was Ferdinand and who later became an intimate friend of mine.

"He was a fencing master.... His mother had died early. His father was a butcher in Strassburg, a notable drinker, and when in 1870 war broke out he joined the French army as purveyor of meat, leaving the boy to shift for himself. Ferdinand was then eight years old. Dressed in shirt and trousers, barefooted, he strayed about the city, through forbidden streets, where nobody would have ventured to leave the house, where they hid in cellars or had fled to trains, where bullets flew right and left.

"Soon he became known everywhere as 'The ballproof youngster' and was sent with a basket to the stores to buy victuals for other. Finally a ropemaker took pity on him and employed the boy for two pieces of bread per day, one at noon and evening, to turn his wheel.

"This vagabond life suited Ferdinand. He wouldn't have asked for anything better. But when the Germans took the city and his identity had been ascertained, it was goodbye Strassburg and independence. He was assigned to an uncle in Basel.

"This uncle was a wealthy business man, but as great a miser as his brother had been drinker and he begrudged the money to educate the boy. He took him in his business and made him work all day.

"When Ferdinand was fifteen years old he found a benefactor who sent him to school, and in one year he made all of the grades and graduated as the first of his class. Later he found employment in a hotel as waiter and from there received a position in London, in a place where many magnificent Jewish weddings were held and everything under the sun was being served.

"At one of those weddings the bill of the cellar didn't balance. Much more wine had been given out than served. So the proprietor called the police and searched and, of the two hundred waiters all but Ferdinand had champagne bottles in their trunks. They were discharged and he was promoted to a departmental chief. With that the greatest opportunities were open to him. He received employment in a hotel frequented by King Edward, where the smallest tip was a pound. One could dine there only by ordering a room in advance. Nothing went back to the kitchen. . . . There are many places in Europe where that is the case, where waiters support several families with what is left over. . . . He made from 60 to 80 pounds a day and could have made a fortune in ten years. But now he is again a poor devil.

"Destiny didn't favor him any more; he grew nervous, suffered from loss of memory and could no longer control his twenty waiters. They cheated him.

"With his savings he then tried everything that doctors and medicine could offer, from Swiss pills to the electric belt. But he didn't regain his health.

"He had become groom of the chamber and by chance found an old book by some obscure author wherein it said that one had to begin every cure, whichever it may be, with three days fasting. That he did, and asserts that after that time he was entirely well, rid of all nervousness.

"It enthused him so that he at once gave up his position, left his electric apparatus and two trunks full of books and travelled home. Only in Wiesbaden he stopped to regard from his new viewpoint the many people who seek their salvation from the waters. Someone on crutches came his way and Ferdinand said to him: 'I know something that will heal you. But I shall tell you about it only if you promise to follow my advice.'

"'I promise,' agreed the stranger.

"'Fast!' ordered Ferdinand.

"After two days he saw the rheumatic sufferer again. He felt better, and in two more days the man was well. Ferdinand was banished from the town.

"He went to Basel where an uncle was master of fencing, learned the trade, and the city gave him a position with a future pension. However, his enthusiasm for fasting was so great that he gave lectures. Even churches in Basel were open to his purpose.

"Of course, if one represents a thing like that he invites prosecution. One Sunday Ferdinand had put up a sign in the fencing hall saying that he was going to fast seven days and then give a lecture about: Christ, the great physician in history.

"Naturally, everybody came to see him weakened by seven days fasting, if for nothing else. But the result was that, beside his fencing, he was urged to lecture regularly. And if somewhere there was a sick being whom nobody could help, he took refuge with Ferdinand, whose slogan was: fast and pray. That, he said, contains all the teachings of healing, but the fasting is most important. In a short time he had a certain name and reputation, so that hardly a day passed without the call for his help, by telegram and every other way.

"The doctors of medicine naturally didn't like that, and so the police forbade him the fencing hall. He wasn't even permitted to accept voluntary admission, and finally, through a friend who was police commissary, was turned out of the city.

"His reputation as doctor of fasting followed him. He learned to know a publisher of a journal called 'Protection of Man.' And one day it brought an article about Ferdinand, entitled: 'A New, Healing Christ,' written so that it came like a bomb to opponents as well as friends. Soon Ferdinand was the most sought and talked of person in Switzerland. It was officially stated that he healed people of all kinds of disease, among them a woman who had suffered from kidney trouble for twenty-nine years.

"In Zurich they brought to him a blind man with the result that he himself began to lecture three months later, his sight restored through fasting.... Everybody in Switzerland and surroundings sought healing from him.

"Morningstar, a Jew, sat in his chair in Basel. He saw that there was something to be gotten from all this—one could make a business of it. Ferdinand only accepted love offerings.

"So he, Morningstar, received people and said: 'Ferdinand is no longer here, but I can do all that he can.' And he took in the cash and developed his routine so that one patient wrote him out a check of sixty thousand marks wherewith to build a sanitarium. He bought a farm near Basal, and in two years had sent the sixty thousand marks to the devil. The police took him up, and that brought Ferdinand, whose name was connected with it, into bad light.

"He opened later another school of fencing, elsewhere, and lived there for twenty-five years, always trying his healing, but doctors and police again and again made trouble for him. I myself employed him finally as assistant, and today he is occupied at a reform sanitarium.

"In Basel the police once had him in the insane asylum, where his case was diagonised as 'fixed ideas,'" said Mr. Ehret, laughing. "His own relatives denied him. But, unfortunately, he didn't have any money, therefore the doctors declared him healthy. When they accused him of having a fixed idea he replied: 'My ideas are fixed indeed! Yours are so worthless that you change them every day. Mine are as sound as the one's who said: 'Heaven and earth shall pass away but my words shall not pass away.''"

Solemnly Mr. Ehret concluded: "His whole aspect was noble. He never in his life had lied.... Such an ideal being grew from a child half-starved, without education, father or mother. Truly: 'Blessed are the poor, for the kingdom of heaven is theirs.'"

Later he told me:

"It was a clear, hot day in July—not a fleck in the sky, when people went to the cemetery. Hundreds of beings who took an interest in Ferdinand and his family participated in this funeral. The weather was so fine that nobody had brought an umbrella.

"As the coffin was lowered the clergyman made a touching speech, and when finished Ferdinand was going to give an address—a thing contrary to all custom and not even permissable.... With personalities of great renown an acquaintance may speak, but here——. Well, he began his speech, but the words stuck in his throat. He only spoke one sentence and that not wholly to the end. It was something like this:

"'In reality I am the murderer of my son, for I was responsible for his existence——.'

"The clergyman interrupted him with a sign of warning, motioned to him to be silent. It was a painful situation. Then a strange thing happened.

"The preacher, during his speech, had the people so
fascinated that nobody was aware of an impending
heavy thunder storm, and when the coffin was being
lowered the first crash came from heaven, cutting off
Ferdinand's words. The next moment a cloud-burst-
like rain fell and the panic-stricken people fled to the
cemetery chapel. In another moment the grave was
full of water and the coffin floated above."

"At that time I lectured," said Mr. Ehret, "and once,
in Stuttgart, the staff-physician came to me after the
lecture, saying that only now he has learned the
value of fasting. But to one thing he objected: That I
am still a bachelor.

"A giggling went through the hall. I told him: 'The
one stipulation is missing. The woman does not exist
as yet. She must not know a thing about cooking.'"

I teased: "Difficult, then, for love to go through the
stomach."

He blustered: "That is the most absurd phrase in
existence. There is a tragedy at the bottom.

"An acquaintance of mine, a poet and leader of the
vegetarian movement, went to New York and there
married a German girl. He had for years lived on fruit
and coarse bread, but now the dear woman again
cooked for him. One day he became sick with
pneumonia and died. She returned to Germany and
married another vegetarian, an officer, who had his
finger amputated because it was crooked. The wound
wouldn't heal for two years. I advised him to fast, and
in six days it was healed up.

"The elderly couple took a fasting cure and became young again. Then the woman said to me, amid tears: 'Now I know that I have cooked my first husband to death.'

"We all are killing each other off as best we can," Mr. Ehret reflected, "and that is well. New life brings new ideas. Think of the many people whose minds have grown stale and rusty with age from lack of usage. Think of the brains that need sweeping and putting in order like some dirty room. But the people are so well satisfied with what they have stored up that nothing but death can change them.... 'One can not put new wine into old bottles.'"

# 15

# The Barefoot Lancer

"I went to Nizza on the Riviera," he continued, "and there I learned to know another singular being from home. Barefooted, without hat, his hair long, he walked along the Promenade des Anglais, creating great excitement. He differed from so-called beings of nature through his cleanliness and display of wealth. An ordinary tramp naturally is supposed to be poor, but he, to refute this, wore several diamond rings and a large jewel stick-pin in the collar of his sailor suit of white silk. He had a certain aristocratic bearing.

"As I passed him he spoke to me, having recognized me from a picture in my book on fasting.* He told me his story.

*These photos of himself during various stages of his Life are to be found in Ehret's "Instructions for Fasting and Dieting." Order direct from Ehret's publisher—Benedict Lust Publications P.O. Box 404, New York, N.Y. 10156 ($2.95 + 75¢ handling)

"An officer of the guards by the lancers in Bonn—one of the finest of regiments—he became ill, and after the usual maltreatment of doctors, got hold of my book. He made a flight.

"A fortune from four to five million marks being at his disposal, he dressed in gala the following day, went to his regiment and resigned from service. Then, in the environs of Berlin, he bought himself a little summer house, stuffed it full of fruit, left the clothes from his body and lived there.

"None of his friends were to visit him. If they came he looked through a window and said: 'I am naked. If that disturbs you go elsewhere.' They believed him to be unbalanced, of course, but within a year he was well.

"Twice he was arrested for walking barefooted along Friedrichstrasse, and after being kept at the police station over night regained his freedom only by the skill of a lawyer and heavy money.

"Now, because of his attire, Hotel des Anglais denied him admission. So he played the following trick: He dressed elegantly and went back, saying he wished to dine there. Then he rode up with a two-horse team and lackey. But when he wanted to have the servant at his table there again was trouble and he first had to change the man's clothes.

"He ordered a bottle of the best wine to be had and that for the lackey. He himself didn't take a drop, neither ate he anything of the previously ordered ten franc dinner but fruit. The guests and waiters were amazed and didn't hesitate to say that he surely is insane, for how can one pay so much for a dinner and then let it pass by?

"Another time he wanted to take a small trip by train, and because he was barefooted they refused to sell him a first-class ticket. So he bought a whole compartment.

"How he enjoyed vexing people. I told him to make better use of his money, to spread the teaching, that with his way of living he only harmed us all. But he laughed and tried to persuade me to go with him to India, where he said people know how to live. When I refused he went alone, travelling through the whole country with a team of oxen. After two years he had reached the other side and wrote from there. Then nothing more was heard of him except that his relatives were quarreling about his fortune."

"No sense of responsibility, no sympathy for others. Those kind of people should be made to work," said I.

Mr. Ehret shook his head, sadly: "I was the one who should have taken the responsibility to turn him into the right path. He was a splendid being. We are all too absorbed in our own affairs."

# 16

# The Entrance to Paradise

"There were now three of us," Mr. Ehret told again, returning to that first spiritualistic meeting with Ferdinand and the other friend. "We soon had different results. A deception could no longer be feared. We proved in the course of our meetings that mediums were not needed, that friends and kindred gladly put themselves in communication with us if we give them a hearing. The most convincing and instructive revelations were those of my own father.

"Above all, he taught me that the world to come isn't anything but the present, except that there is no concrete matter, bound to space and time. He asserted that he himself was dwelling in wonderful spheres of light and soon would no longer be able to come to the cold and dark atmosphere of the earth, to us, where unblessed spirits abide.

"Most surprising was his statement that he never had met my mother in the hereafter, that evidently she dwelt in spheres to which he didn't gravitate. One day he reported that he was striving heavenward.

"But, what is heaven?" we asked.

"There came those very concise words: 'Light. Eternal light.'

"All men have to go there and do not come to rest until they are there. Till now, however, it has been possible only for Christ to go there directly," Mr. Ehret stated. I didn't know if that too was a revelation from his father or his own conviction, and didn't ask.

"Often I have been called a dreamer," he went on to say, "and once I had a dream, a foreboding, that a great war was to come. I advised my sister and brother-in-law to move to Switzerland. They went, and bought a beautiful country estate near Askona. I myself intended to establish a sanitarium there later.

"In those days there went through the paper the news that a certain archduke of Austria, who had studied in Zurich and then resigned his heritage to the throne, married the well known Adamowitzsch. She was a singer, a beauty, and it was said that she had joined a society of natural healing.

"With the article there was this picture: A board-fence and back of it a fruit garden. On the door was written: 'The Entrance to Paradise.' The archduke and his bride were pictured as original beings clad in skins, nearing the door where the owner stood presenting the little couple with an apple. This, it said, is the reception.

"Now, the aim of the paper was to make ridicule of the affair. It stated even that Adamowitzsch walked about naked, with hair hanging loose, that she no longer bathes and that her husband therefore intended to divorce her.

"In reality there was nothing like it. A few, peaceful people had joined upon the fundamental and with the ideal of a bloodless, vegetarian diet. The bloodless they emphasized especially. The mountain upon which this colony originated was baptized Monte Verita: mountain of truth. The archduke with his bride and a friend were there only a short time and dressed elegantly. All else was lies.

"Another illustrated magazine likewise brought a sensational report exuberant with vulgarity and falsehoods, so that an official complaint was made against it. It had to bring a counter-article or be sued for damage.... The press is the most responsible institution of today.

"The founder of this colony was a rich Belgian who intended to build the affair upon a communistic basis. The main ideal was strict vegetarianism. Originally fruit was to be eaten only. An Englishman who wanted fried potatoes had to leave.... But, as in many other cases, the communistic idea eventually was the dissolution of the organization. It became a signal for certain idlers.

"However, this didn't diminish my enthusiasm to establish a colony on a similar basis. And at any rate, the beautiful and idyllic village situated on the Lago Maggiore obtained thereby a universal reputation. It is a fisher village with undefiled, naive people, still uncorrupted by culture.

"In time there came travellers from all parts of the world to see this remarkable organization, which in the meanwhile had dissolved. Today Askona is a center of attraction for tourists. They come from everywhere, seeking truth and deliverance. How my eyes and imagination used to follow them up Monte Verita and its small bungalows, where, because of its mysterious attraction, the previous owner opened an air bath and charged two francs admission.

"The most variegated assemblage. Russian anarchists, students, clergymen who despaired about the truth, the poor, the rich, all united by the one idea: Where *is* truth? Finally, among the antagonists, Monte Verita was called the mount of falsehood.

"All the nationalities. One heard every language under the sun, as if the little fisher village were some great universal city. It had something fictitious. Still, everything breathed peace, satisfaction, and one could never imagine that any being with evil thoughts should linger there.

"There then, I established my home. And there Hilda came to me. There also I had my first patient.

"In the evening, out upon the terrace, by twilight and gigantic mountains, one lost the hunger for all else.

"In the course of time my colony became the most interesting thing there. So many visitors came that I had to lock my house-door. Now I am two years away and still every other day someone comes to visit me. I finally wrote on the door that one could speak to me only after having announced himself by mail.

"Personally I stepped into a certain contrast to those beings of nature, but partly they became my friends. O the gypsyness about them! Outwardly they will make a show of naturalness, while on the inside they are far from it.

"This colony does no longer exist. I too had to learn from experience that communistic ideas are not practical in the world of today.

"One of the most interesting members of our organization was a brilliant author by the name of Englehart. He caused much talk because he had bought himself a whole island in Cabocon, Bismark Archipelago, and dwelt there several years editing a journal titled, 'Sun, Coconut and Grapes.' The natives working in his plantation received their daily wage in coconut, there being no money in the place.

"He grew very homesick, for nobody would come to him, not even his bride. There had been a controversy about him in the Vegetarian Ward for three, four,

perhaps five or six years. He issued an appeal that
settlers, able to meet their own travelling expenses,
could live with him free of charge. He was the only
being taking this step in a thousand years. However,
he met with no success. Even people ready to venture
almost anything hesitated because of the fever
prevailing there. And he himself was honest enough
to state that he still suffered from eruptions.

"Finally one man took a chance, a highly gifted and
celebrated musician of the West, the leader of an
orchestra. He went there for an ideal, to prove that
vegetarianism could withstand the fever. He died.

"That, of course, discouraged fearfully. Afterwards
the author sent two people the money to come, and
they also died.

"I nearly came going myself. It seemed as if destiny
gave me a wink. Always I had longed for such a
blessed isle with sun and fruit, away from the throng
of people and their crowded dwellings. I wrote an
article saying that one had to fast in Berlin if he
wished to be Cabocon proof, not wait until there.

"But this man, like every other prophet, had a hobby
which saved me from taking the fatal step. He
asserted that coconut was the only fruit to eat, that
one should live on it. 'There is so much nourishment
in a single coconut that a being could live on it for a
week,' he said.

"Today he is still alone and writes about the happy
life he is leading there."

# 17

# Convincing Experiences at a Spiritualism Meeting

"Tell me how you met Hilda in Askona," I begged, when he had no more to say.

"She came to the meeting," he replied simply.

"Dead?"

"If you will have it thus." Then: "It was on the summit of a mount, in a little home, a bungalow. Several of my friends were there. A spirit came, calling itself Hilda. It turned out that she was my former friend. Not knowing that she had passed away, I asked why she was here instead of with her child and husband. And she replied: 'The spirits dwell among those whom they love.'

"Then she went on to say that she had been at my lecture in Munich and described the hall. Remarkable and very convincing was that she declared to have died in a certain hospital in a certain city, and when inquiring there I learned that it was true.

"At a second meeting she said that two souls belonging together will have to meet, even if only in some hereafter. True marriages are made in heaven.... I asked how her health was now, and she said that she still has to cough."

When expressing my surprise at this, Mr. Ehret said: "The first patient who came to me in Askona was an architect known for building many beautiful residences in Stockholm. He had consumption in the highest degree besides another suspicious disease. He died even before fasting half a day.

"Now, he too came to the meeting and told that he is still ailing in the hereafter, and when I asked him why he did not move the table more vigorously, he said: 'How can I? You know that my right arm is lame.'"

Grinning broadly, Mr. Ehret told about an old friend whose greatest pleasure was eating and drinking the best, who didn't mind walking an hour to where he could get the desired good meal. "According to my opinion his hell in the hereafter will be an eternal desire for food and drink but no gratification," he concluded. "The hereafter has no lies and no money. The spirits, the glorified bodies can see through each other."

It was in some select society, but all the seats were taken and the place darkened when we arrived so that we had to get camping chairs and place them as best we could. Later, in the light, I saw that but one woman was among us, and that was I; that all were learned-looking men, mostly bald and spectacled, and that Mr. Ehret had managed to find a seat among them.

Afterwards I told him how well he fitted in with that group of people in spite of his saying that he didn't belong among the learned. He corrected me: "I said that I would never go to them for wisdom."

"Oh," answered I, carelessly, "who is wise——"

"Those who are enthusiastic about living," said he.

"The learned try to banish that enthusiasm, religion does, and yet all of the saviors have taught it. We should be so enthusiastic about life that it impresses us like a vivid dream."

"You have experienced it?"

"At times. When first I regained my health I knew how thrilling life could be, the mere knowledge of existence. One can't appreciate a gift of something one never missed. Health doesn't seem such a precious possession to people who haven't ever been sick. But I, when coming back from Nizza, able to take up my position again, was tipsy with the joy of being!

# 18

# From Suicide to Resurrection through Fasting

"With the adoption of the Kneipp treatment I had turned my back on medicine and sought healing in Nature. My groping was to become entirely well. This I did with strict vegetarianism, eating hardly anything but fruit.

"However, my relatives made evil charges against my way of living, and since I still believed in the one mistake, the drinking of milk, they gradually won me back to the old habits.

"When for the first time I appeared again at the restaurant for luncheon my friends embraced me with loud cheer. Now, they thought, I behaved once more like a sane being. My great change had been a hindrance to our friendship.

"But, this false glory lasted about half a year and then I had the old story over again. My kidney pains returned.

"I went to Algiers. On the steamer a missionary from India sat next to me, eating nothing of the whole dinner but the apple cake. Greatly interested, I asked: 'Don't you ever eat more?' He replied merrily: 'Anything you eat is quite useless tonight.'

"He was dressed like a Capuchin, but in white. 'I am from South-India,' he explained later, 'the only part free from the English, and there we have the fever. One has to abstain from much food.'"

Mr. Ehret smiled broadly, reflectively. Then pulling his wide-brimmed hat low over his forehead, as if he were still walking on that steamer, continued: "I awoke during the night. There was my suitcase flying down from the berth above. Such a storm! A waiter entered and asked in French what I wished to have: 'Cognac or ——.' The second word I didn't understand, so I told him to bring me it." He laughed: "The boy brought a board to keep me from falling out of the bed.

"The next day I couldn't go to the dining room but was told that ropes had been drawn along the tables to hold the dishes. The following morning, while dressing, the waiter called to me: 'Venez voir Alger!' (Come and see Algiers.)

"A picture of delight, this aspect of the city. Snow-white buildings, the deep blue ocean. Those oriental houses are all flat roofed, each a poem in itself. Other people, different clothing, another world. And back of it the large, dark green forest. It was October and an agreeable warmness lay above it all.

"A former pupil of mine got off the ship. Later I visited him daily. The boy was ill. Once upon a time he had shown a hatred for all that was connected with the church or God.

"'Prove to me that there is an all-knowing Deity,' he had said. 'He would have to be either powerless or cruel to tolerate the blind suffering and injustice of this world. It is a falsehood, an invention of worldly rulers to make us easy subjects.'

"I argued that we were given a will to choose. He laughed derisively: 'The will is a faculty very unevenly distributed and subject to other faculties, and some of us were born with precious few.'

"'We each have received the all-powered faculty of love,' argued I.

"'The world has been dripping with so-called love for two thousand years and not profited anything,' he replied wearily.

"His parents were rich people. The father brought the now highly consumptive young man to the finest hospital. When there I pressed his hand in farewell and said: 'Until we meet again in some future world.' To my surprise he answered: 'Yes, if it is the will of God.'

"Sickness, the uncertainty of life had taught him better.

"Those Arabians," said Mr. Ehret in another strain, "those natives of whom the most terrible tales are told—what are they? The whole East threatens Europe with the yellow peril, it is said. Yet there is nothing but religious danger, for none of us have learned as yet to stand secure.

"They are a sincere race, with only one book: the Koran, their Bible; no culture otherwise—nothing. And when the Koran says: 'Thou shalt not cheat,' they don't cheat. In Constantinople, where it would be an easy matter to deceive, there being so many languages and nationalities, the Arab deals with you in strict honesty.

"I first visited their churches. They are absolutely empty of pictures and altars, nevertheless they impressed me deeply because of their beauty of architecture. The floors are covered with costly rugs. The colored windows give a wonderful light. Before putting a foot inside you have to take off your shoes.

"Our Christians could learn something if they ever saw those Arabian men at prayer. (I do not mention women because one rarely sees them; they ride in closed vehicles.) While the priest prays upon the stage those men stand like soldiers, bowing only to each prayer while he kisses the floor towards East, to Mecca, the grave of Mohammed. There is an indescribable grace in all of their movements. When acquaintances meet in the street each touches his forehead and chest as a greeting, and intimate friends embrace and kiss.

"In Algiers I was thrown together with people who hadn't any learning or culture, yet their manner, their grace was something inexpressibly fine.

"The greatest surprise was their casbah—the market. It usually is the most narrow built quarter of the city, with stores partly in the street. Such an overwhelming feeling, so homelike—all of those many colored figures, withal so black. One feels that it ought to be thus in heaven.

"There are many romances and books on travel describing the dangers of Arabia. But I walked through the streets at all hours of the night; I roamed through the forests; nobody hurt a hair on my head.

"From the casbah I went to the better part of the city, up along the mountains, where the residences lay, and there found a furnished room with terrace. The place belonged to a French professor conducting a private school, an amiable man, who at once made me feel at home. The street was named after the inventor of photography, Daguerre. I had a wonderful view—and when it began to rain took a bath out upon the terrace. It comes down so warm and turns all of the streets into rivulets in a few minutes.

"My food there was manderins and Morocco dates, still hanging on their branches, the way the Arabians sell them in the street. I felt so well thereby that at times it seemed that I could fly. But the next day

the reverse was possible. This contrast from whole-
ness, strength and intellectual freedom to the depths
of despair brought me down to the ocean one day,
where I walked up and down considering if I should
jump into the water or end it all in some other way,
when the idea of starvation came.

"'Why not?' I thought. I was a mere skeleton now. It
wouldn't take long. I went home and for the next
three days lay in bed like a corpse, except that I didn't
sleep and dreamed of hell.... But who knows," he
laughed, "but what that also might happen after one
is dead?... During the night, from the sixth to the
seventh day, however, a deep sleep came upon me,
and when on the following morning the Oriental sun
smiled warmly in on my bed I jumped out with one
leap, feeling that the supernatural power of a new life
ran through my veins instead of death. So strong I
felt that I was urged to try my new power on
something, and lifted up the dresser. Then, still
exuberant, I took my bicycle and rode without
stopping to the city Blieta, forty-two kilometers
away.

"It is called the land of golden fruit and is glorious.
Passing the manderin fields I refreshed myself on
their gifts and rode back again. After my eighty-four
kilometers trip I felt even better than before. The idea
of suicide through starvation had failed me.

# 19

# My First Patient

"I knew that one should not eat too much even of fruit, and so now I ate only once a day and felt increasingly better and grew stronger and stronger. Then I planned to return home not in the old way but cross northern Africa to Tunis and come back through Italy.

"This, of course, I didn't wish to do alone. So I wrote to several friends to join me, but none would come."

He smiled: "I remembered a proof of thought power of many years past, when a volunteer in Munich. All of my money was gone by the first of the month and my new allowance hadn't arrived. It was a morning in July and I had to go to the barracks at five o'clock, but didn't have a penny wherewith to buy breakfast. I thought: 'Never in your life have you found anything. Could not now heaven open itself?' And I sent up a sincere, short prayer. Then, looking to the ground—I hardly trust my eyes—I see a fifty pfennig piece there upon the sidewalk.

"This I remembered now, and so every night when going to bed I lay down with the feeling that some friend would be reached by my thoughts. I had grown mentally stronger and believed this to be possible. And behold, after a few days there came a postal from a friend of whom I never had thought, a sportsman, saying he should like to take a trip with me through the southern countries by wheel. I wrote him to come, and in four or five days he was there. Just the companion I wanted. I couldn't have wished for a better."

"That widely praised Algerian wine," Mr. Ehret told another time. "I didn't touch it. But my friend one day came home in a merry condition, and putting a bottle before me on the table, said: 'Unless you drink this ere we leave Algiers I will no longer be your friend. You deserve a beating.'

"He grinned: I drank it. It was the best I ever tasted. Like gold it looked. One could take it to be olive oil when pouring. It had the scent of roses, lovely, sweet and almost without alcohol. Moscat doux des Pères Blancs, it was called, after a trappist order, the Pères Blancs, also known as the White Fathers.

"Those Pères Blancs have a great privilege in living in the land where the white wine grows: it is theirs and grows all about their cloisters. Fermented without alcohol, they send it all over Europe as mass-wine.

"My friend and I made an excursion and spent a night with the Trappists to learn to know one of their cloisters and also because of the wine. It is now the only order of the Catholic church who practice the virtues of Christianity to perfection. A fleshless diet, fasting and silence. Only at certain hours they may converse.... 'Let your conversation be yes, yes, and no, no.'

"We were received by the only monk who was allowed to speak. A splendid dinner was served, the best part of which was the absence of chatter. They take no pay and do not ask about one's religion. Everybody is welcome.

"Long before arriving at the cloister one is met by a delicious fragrance. It comes from the camomile fields surrounding the place and fills the air at many miles distance. They provide all France with ca-momile. Oh, to sleep by the open window at night, inhaling this odor!"

"The dinner," I asked. "What was it?"

Mr. Ehret had to think. "Each of the monks had a simple bowl made of zinc," he said then. "In this he received some soup. A piece of brown bread and two apples lay by the side."

"And the cloister?"

"The most remarkable part about that was the cellar. A lay-brother showed us around. It was cemented like a swimming pool, only instead of water it was filled with red wine. In the fall, at harvest time, if the old wine isn't used up they let it flow into the brook.

"A great ideal is brought to realization in such a cloister: no quarrels, no inharmony; everybody has his duties; all work. It is practical Christianity. Well they knew why they surrounded each cloister with a wall. For back of those walls, away from the curious eyes of the world, the foundation was laid for all that we have today of valuable literature and art."

The question of the cellar not being settled with me as yet I asked why they didn't put the old wine into bottles instead of letting it run away.

"It is too cheap for that," replied Mr. Ehret absently, having already gone back to Algiers. A picture there caused his face to light up.

"One meets such remarkable sincere people!" he said. "An elderly gentleman, a neighbor—fine, upright soul—evidently had got the impression that I was religious. Finding me once in a dreary mood, he looked intently into my face and said: 'My friend, have you given any time to your God today?' I had to confess that I hadn't. He told me to go and do so, that I would return with a better light. I did.

"Coming back, I wrote down my experiences from suicide to resurrection. My friend later helped me to translate it into good French, and brought it to an

editor of a French paper in Cairo. He was so enthused
about it that on the following day he came to me with
a nearly blind friend. He was a rich Arabian and
believed that I could help him. This was my first
patient, and among all the one who took the matter
with intense seriousness. I advised him to fast and he
wrote me out a check for five-thousand francs.
Through this opportunity I was introduced to his
family and so gained entrance into an Arabian
house, something very difficult to get, especially for a
European.

"He still wore the familiar red cap which they never
take off, not in the home, street or church, not at
greetings nor at court. It is even being whispered that
they keep it on in bed.... A rather corpulent man, this
patient of mine. His wife was a slender Turkish
beauty clad in Parisian fashion.

"In the middle of their house was the parlor and
sitting room in one, large as a dance-hall, without
table or chairs, but deep divans all along the walls.
They still had the custom of sitting on the floor. Doors
led from this place to all of the different surrounding
rooms and sleeping chambers. I was told that all
Arabian houses are built like that.

"A black entered and passed mocha upon a board,
candy and cigarets. Now, this Arabian began his fast
with greatest enthusiasm, and one fine day arrived at
my place with the editor and two wonderful gray
horses. He said that there was a remarkable
improvement in his sight, beginning already on the
tenth day.

"On the following day, when I again visited his house, a strange scene met me. His wife received me with tears. Naturally, I thought that something had happened to her husband. Her gestures indicated that he was absent. She didn't speak a word of any European language, but was withall very amiable, when suddenly the little flapper of a daughter came in from school, where she was learning French.

"'Has some evil befallen your father?' I questioned her, "since your mother weeps.'

"She didn't know and had to ask her, and then as well as her poor French would permit, she gave me to understand that her father had so wonderfully changed since his fast. Whereas, formerly he always sat drinking at the tavern he now remains at home and is sensible. Those were tears of joy.

"But," Mr. Ehret laughed, ruefully, "now a verse from Schiller is befitting: 'With the powers of destiny no eternal tie is to be woven, for misfortune travels fast.'

"At the same moment, while the woman tearfully showed me her joy, the husband came into the room, quite drunk, dancing and making speeches, telling that he had once more visited his boon-companions. His brother followed and gave him a piece of his mind.... That was the end of that affair."

# 20

# The Homeward Journey Begins

"Large mountains, and I climbing upward," said Mr. Ehret. "That was my dream during the night before my friend arrived. And climbing meaning good fortune, we started in the blithest of spirits, like two youngsters into fairyland.

"Our first destiny was the city Setif. Its streets were a wonderful surprise to us, not because of any special beauty or sordidness, but for their absence of noise and traffic. My friend was so delighted with it that he kept saying: 'I must take this trip again with my wife; she would appreciate this.'

"Everything was very inexpensive. We lived in the best hotel for two francs a day. They are usually Italian or French, but the Frenchman has the

advantage over his Italian brother, for if one asks
him: Have you a good room for two francs he always
says yes, whereas the other will stick to strict rules.
For a few pennies they will set enough fruit and
honey before you for several meals.

"It was Sunday, and a special holiday among the
natives, a socalled Italian night, so when the sun
went down we received another surprise: the quiet
city woke up. Such splendor! Those festive gowns and
decorations appearing suddenly, the music. One
believed to be living through the fable of Thousand
and One Nights.

"I spied a youth sitting in a doorway, leaning
listlessly against the wall. I thought he was asleep
when a woman, evidently his mother, appeared
asking in French if he was ill. 'Where is Marie?' she
asked them. 'Marie,' the boy acknowledged sadly,—
'she has kissed another.'

"Youth is the most tragic time of life," reflected Mr.
Ehret. Then he went on to describe how the following
day they steered in direction of the famous oasis city
Biska and for the first time found themselves in the
desert.

"How excited we were!" he said. It is like seeing the
ocean for the first time. The night was so cold that we
hardly could hold the handle of our wheels, and
withall so silent. No soft grass, no water ditch,
nothing but sand, and here and there a sapling blown
about by the winds. If we too placed ourselves in the
cold and drought instead of the sheltered life we lead
we should possess the fine durability of the sapling.

"Most impressive were the wonderful violet shades of sky and earth. I used to think that the artists were swindling when they produced those beautiful colors where there is nothing but sand and air. But now I saw that the splendor was real.

"The next place was about ninety kilometers away and my friend, whom I will call Peter, said that if something happens to our wheels we shall have to walk all night and the following day. We had plenty of fruit along and Peter some good wine, so another night beneath the sky had only one terror, the cold. Fate, however, smiled on us and in the evening led us to a little village.

"There the whole curious-eyed community gathered about us at once. They never had seen a bicycle, the officer examining our passports explained, hence this excitement.

"This entire oasis, consisting of a little village, has only one fountain as water supply, but it bubbles up, a wide shaft, large as a pillar. Some ancestors of a certain widow discovered the well, and so she has the only right to have a water pipe put into her yard. Every other villager has to fetch his supply with a bucket. It is delightful to drink, and one wonders why in this wilderness, without a tree or bush, such a powerful well should be. As far as it reaches there is grass.

"We went to the only hotel and that, because of its broken windows, looked suspicious. So when the proprietress informed us that all of the rooms were taken by the post that was to come through that evening, we weren't sorry. But there we stood, not knowing which way to turn.

"By chance a noble looking man with his family passed by, the major, and him I asked if there wasn't any possibility of finding shelter over night, and he said that we should sleep in his barn. Then I happened to think of the influential widow who owned the well. And there we went and were given the spare room with the remark: 'Don't be afraid of anything. My husband was murdered in here last week. He won't bother you.'

"We went to bed with uneasy feelings, and for the first time Peter put a revolver under his pillow. The following morning we hurried again like mad through the hot desert and about twelve o'clock reached the railroad station. When you see a locomotive in such a place you appreciate that piece of culture, and think that civilization isn't such a bad thing after all.

"We put in a new supply of fruit and Peter went to dine at the inn while I visited the horse market. There were about two thousand horses, splendid to look at, and several of their Arabian owners. I was the only European. And the thought came to me: 'Why do all of those animals look alike—for it would have been difficult to trace any certain one that was lost in the crowd—and why do men, born and raised in the same climite, differ so greatly?' And like a shot the answer came: 'Animals live by instinct; man by will.'

"As a child I often had wondered why we had been given a will and were supposed to choose right from wrong with the promise of punishment if choosing the wrong, when unable to always discern one from the other. And we are children still, suffering the consequences of wrong discernment. Hence the great cry for compassion."

He said with the enthusiasm of a boy: "The sultan has two magnificent regiments, one all gray, the other all brown horses."

I asked if horses were his favorite animals, and he replied: "They have, of all creatures, the most beautiful, soulful eyes."

"We went to Biska," he continued, "starting at noon. It is one of the largest and most fertile oasis in the desert Sahara, consisting of a large forest of date palms, so fruitful that they supply a big part of Europe with muscat dates. For its growth and fruitfulness the palm needs three elements: sand, glowing sun and water. There are channels going through the whole forest, irrigating the mighty trees, and also ways for traffic, and footpaths. This Biska is a health resort with the finest of weather all winter long. No storms, no rain.

"We arrived at a hotel that was a veritable flower garden. Flowers all over the entrance, the yard, the stairway, the hall. Everywhere beautiful, violet and red flowers. And everything was buzzing with bees, but nobody was afraid of them.

"In the evening we visited some sort of a theater where the natives perform their dances, and on the following day continued our journey.

"It took us across the Atlas mountains. We must have already seen them, coming from Setif, but took them to be clouds. And now, before stepping on the mountain road, we anticipated spending the night in a so-called cart-man's hotel. The place, however, was so full of bed-bugs that they chased us out of the feathers at twelve o'clock at night. Fortunately. Before us was fairyland itself, so interwoven with brooks and bridges and the bright moonlight falling upon it.

"We pushed our wheels up through the forest. Below they had told us that leopards and monkeys are still living there. Yet we heard and saw nothing but a driver, who called to us from the distance: 'Bosure messieurs!'

"At day-break we were at a sunny height, and Peter hungrily regarded a ham-sandwich. 'There, now,' he said, 'if friend leopard comes he shall have half of it.' But friend leopard didn't come, and we lay down in the sun to sleep."

"Supposing he had come." I gasped.

Mr. Ehret smiled philosophically: "Weren't we sleeping the sleep of contentment? If death were to come I would rather he found me there, at the height of happiness, than in the depth of despair." And he talked some more about the charms of the street, its tunnels and bridges, calling it one of the most memorable ones in the world.

"We passed a sign board," he said, "whereupon was written that a certain French general had, with several regiments, built this street in the astonishingly short time of thirty-six days, for the only aim of bringing the canons up there, where the Cabylen dwell, is to make them submissive to his government.

"Those Cabylen are a colored tribe, not black, but beautiful beings with soft brown, transparent skin and shining eyes. Their whole country is a chain of little hills. They do not build in the valley, like we, but on mountains. Their little village on the summit looked most original.

"I once was told by a gentle old man that being bossed by another race was like being horsewhipped, but one didn't mind it so much since the one who handled the whip couldn't know what he was doing. And yet we call ourselves civilized and Christians and regard those people as savages.

"We didn't see that Cabylen village until the following day," he continued. "After our sleep on the height we again took to our wheels, and in a little inn by the road were told that we couldn't possibly get across the high pass because the way is still many feet under snow.

"This was really so, but we wouldn't take the warning. There was a little water-fall before the snow began, and in it we took a bath to strengthen ourselves. A ravine was towards the north. As we were going to step across it someone called in a thundering voice that resounded from the rocks: 'Turn! For you shall not get through!'

"We then noticed three Arabians on the other side, and Peter said: 'They are one too many. If they attack us——'

"But I answered the Arabian, shouting through my hands: 'Thank you. We shall get through.' We shouldered our wheels and carried them across the white barricade, a distance of about two miles. It took us an hour. Then we sat down and gratefully ate our oranges and some snow.

"The monkey forest lay below and we had to pass through it, but didn't encounter a monkey. It was now four o'clock in the afternoon and Peter remarked that we are still seventy kilometers from the next station that was to be reached before night, since we hadn't any lanterns. He always was keen about mileage and time. Luckily, as the forgetting of those things is one of my weaknesses.

"We hurried, yet darkness found us still on the road, congratulating ourselves, though, because of its smoothness. Suddenly we lay on a heap of stone. Peter swore. The street was newly gravelled but not rolled. Our riding had come to an end.

"We had pushed our wheels, as best we could, alongside of the forest for some time when I smelled smoke and saw a faint, distant light. From the street a large, dark mass emerged of which one's fancy could build an elephant. For a monkey it was too large. However, the thing didn't mean any harm. It turned out to be a gigantic steam roller," chuckled Mr. Ehret. "Now the two of us rejoiced. There must be people dwelling near.

"Presently we came upon a hut and some light. A large dog leaped toward us, yelping fiercely, followed by an astonished man. The place was surrounded by a board fence; a big fire burned within; a kettle hung over the flames and around it people of all colors sat, black, brown and white, preparing the evening meal. Such an artistic aspect. It was the most wonderful picture I ever saw.

"The man coming to meet us was obviously the manager; those others were the workers of the steam-roller. To my question how far the next station was, he replied that it was far and we weren't likely to reach it; we should spend the night with him. 'There is plenty of straw,' he said, meaning for us to sleep in, and he insisted that we sit down among them and eat a bowl of soup.

"I can still see those blacks with their gleaming white teeth and shining eyes relishing their food. Besides soup they each received a piece of meat and bread in their hand.

"But we were anxious to be on our way, and the amiable manager accompanied us as far as the gravel lasted and we again had the large, beautiful street before us. However, only a glimmer of its whiteness was to be seen, night had grown so dark.

"We rode on, not knowing where, until we came to a cross-road, and, says Hebel: 'If you come to a cross-road, ask your conscience; it talks plainly.' But who wouldn't rather have a sign-post? Luckily, there was one, and I climbed up and Peter passed me a match. There it said: 17 kilometers to H——.

"This now was somewhat comforting, and again we took to the road, when suddenly we met a telegraph-post. Usually there also is a railroad. We searched the Baedecker for a hotel, but found it closed. Then an Arabian who came to put out the few street lanterns directed us to a small inn with a beautiful garden in front, and here, too, the proprietor was just going to close the door.

"Everything being under French control there one has to report at each place.... The innkeeper was somewhat drunk. Putting the hotel register before us, he said: 'You can write in it what you please; I shall not betray anything.'"

Mr. Ehret laughed: "He took us for a couple of vagabonds; I presume we looked the part.... I was so tired and thirsty that I drank five or six glasses of lemonade and then became lost to the world until the following day, when we were bound for the north African city, Tunis.

# 21

# Abundant Strength from Dates and Oranges

"This Tunis is a wonderful place," Mr. Ehret went on to say. "While Constantinople and Cairo are rather dirty and no longer genuine, the native quarter in Tunis is still unfalsified, clean, and of picturesque beauty. Going through those streets one finds every house, person and store a fit subject for painting. The pure soul of those people felt by the stranger! I went out walking nights with a consciousness of greater safety than in any city of culture.

"One of the greatest attractions is such an Arabian coffee-house. To sit there upon a bench and straw-mat by a little bamboo table, smoking a cigarette, before you the glowing charcoals in the fireplace where the Arab makes coffee while you wait, is a delight. Coffee and cigarettes play an important role with those people. By taking now and then a piece of bread and a few dates or oranges, beside the cigarette, they perform the hardest of labor.

"In everything the Arab consults the Koran. He washes hands and mouth at a large well, before and after eating, and eats only unleavened bread. His simple way of living interested me much. Those people live on so little and have more strength than the Europeans.

"Coming down from the hotel one morning I met an Arab carrying a large round thing of about three feet in diameter on his head. As he passed me I received the wonderful smell of freshly baked cake. I said to him: 'What have you there?'

"'Cake,' he answered. 'Will you have a piece?'

"'Alright,' said I. And for five centimes he gave me an enormous piece, and it smelled so good that I began to eat in the liveliest of streets. Then, as he ran away, pan on his head, through the dense crowd, I jumped on a car and rode after him, to purchase another piece for Peter. Now, I tried to find out where he got the cake that one may buy some more of it later. But he babbled something about a Turkish bakery; name or street he didn't know.

"I returned to the hotel and gave the piece to Peter. As soon as he tasted it he cried: 'Lord, this is good. If only my wife could have some of it!'

"We at once started out to search, and after two days found the Arab and that Turkish bakery where there was nothing to be had but those cakes and some lemonade made by an Italian, also unusually good because he always put a piece of lemon-peel in it and closed it up tight.

"Peter was bound to get the recipe and send it to his wife. 'She will be tipsy with joy over it,' he said. We walked every day for half an hour to get that cake and still talked about it five or six years later. My friend always sought to induce his wife to take the journey with him to Africa and learn how to make it. Its main ingredients are Turkish barley, first roasted a little and then shredded, some browned almonds and burned sugar. Over the whole a crust of sweet icing is poured. Simple enough, but no baker in all Europe can produce anything like it.

"In Tunis, in the street, at twelve o'clock at night, one may any day find a group of people standing around a man with a little oven, baking those cakes and giving the buyer a spoonful of melted sugar on top.

"Everything in that city is inexpensive and good. Peter, who once in a while grew tired of the fruit diet, dined one evening at an elegant French restaurant. He received a bottle of wine, entree, soup, fish, roast, vegetables, pullet with salad, cake, several kinds of fruit, cheese and coffee, all for one franc and a half.... I bought a hat two francs cheaper than in Milan. And silk is almost given away. Most people are dressed in silk.

"Those cheap prices of food, lodging, clothes, the theater, are the result of French and Italian competition. One can, for instance, go from Marsalla to Tunis for ten francs, third class, while the trip to Naples, which is nearer, costs four times that much.... The Italians have good cause of fearing the loss of Tunis.

"About an hour's distance from there are the ruins of Carthage, the once famous fruit country. Now there remains nothing but large water works and fields of artichokes irrigated through gasoline motor pumps.

"We took the ship from Tunis to Marsalla, the southern end of Sicily, where Italy's best wine grows. A terrible storm raged when we arrived so that we couldn't anchor at the pier; small boats came to take the frightened passengers. Some ladies were so nervous they cried, and the Italians took this opportunity to charge terrible prices. Peter and I, refusing to agree to the robbery, would not leave the ship. Then the captain himself came, and calling a pilot, ordered him to bring us across for fifty cts.

"Now our trip on wheel began again, through the wonderful land Sicily. We rode for days through lemon groves where the trees were so laden that there was more fruit than leaves. Terribly heated up, dusty and tired, we arrived finally in the city Palermo. At the first fruitstand we discovered (usually they are kept by women) we each bought a couple of pounds of nespoli. But where to eat that fruit now? There were no benches, so we began to eat standing in the street.

"At that Peter grew so angry that he threw his whole bag of nespoli at an empty building and went into a restaurant. I," Mr. Ehret laughed, "leaned against the wall and would have finished mine. But Peter came out again in a moment, crying: 'Damn it! Now we are among the robbers of Sicily. I, paying three lire for a meal. If only we had that cake from Tunis!"

"He vanished around the corner. Suddenly he returned with another bag, all smiles this time, and said: 'Try this.'

"He had warm potatoe-vermicellis.

"'Now,' he rejoiced, 'we are fixed again...I have a good mind to go and hold that scamp of a waiter those noodles under his nose. For three lire he wouldn't even show me the bill of fare.... Over there lives an old woman who makes these.'

"I, too, went and bought a bag full of noodles, made of sweet potatoes, and discovered that the main attraction for Peter was not the old woman with her products, but the wine-room before which she sat.

"Such a Sicilian wine-room or tavern is the most poetical thing in existence, as good as its wines of which Peter already had tried a glass. It is at the same time a cellar. The barrels are there where one drinks, piled up against the wall to the ceiling. On every barrel the name of the wine is written, and the vintage. Every glass is drawn directly from the barrel. As in all Italian wine-rooms, the madonna stands pictured in a corner; before her, in a little red lamp burns the eternal light.

"Neither beer or any other kind of liquor is sold in such a place—that would be a desecration of the wine for which the madonna stands as patron-saint. If the keeper would cheat only once she would be taken

from him. She stands for truth, and one may be sure
of receiving genuine wine in her presence, also that
everything is peaceable.

"That there is something holy connected with it all
one can feel as soon as entering the room. The Italian
is known to curse a great deal, yet were he to curse or
use ill language at such a tavern he would receive no
more wine. A certain devotional atmosphere pre-
dominates, a sort of church discipline.

"Peter said that one could not wish for anything
better than such a tavern, that wine and vermicelli.

"The city of Palermo is beautiful, and, as in most
Italian cities, her greatest beauty is her churches.
Unless one has seen those churches of Italy one has
no idea of what can be accomplished in the art of
architecture. It is a nation's expression of
culture.... Some of them there are consisting of only
marble and gold, and the definition artistic is not
sufficient here. Those are master works of human
thought and skill. In our present day we are trying to
belittle all this, are looking down upon the middle
ages, yet are unable by far to accomplish the like.

"The Italian values good music and song.... In those
large churches, whose colored windows, pictures and
flowers alone produce a wonderful atmosphere, there
is always a violin concert on Sunday, Also special
singing, beside the organ music. Such a deep voiced,
vibrant organ is the most beautiful of human
creations. It was the only thing that drew me to
church as a boy."

# 22

# From Palermo to Naples

"Now 'neath the silvermoon ocean is glowing,
   O'er the calm billow soft winds are blowing,
Here balmy zephers blow, pure joys invite us,
   And as we gently row, all things delight us.
Hark how the sailors cry, joyously echoes nigh,
   Santa Lucia, Santa Lucia.
Home of fair poesy, realm of pure harmony,
   San-ta Lu-cia, San-ta Lu-ci-a."

Listening to Mr. Ehret singing that old, beautiful
Neapolitan song upstairs while I prepared supper,
took me back to singers on a steamer in the Pacific.
He often sang for me and had a rich, deep voice.
"But," I teased him later, "they sang that song more

beautiful than you; they had pain in it; you sing it too cheerily."

He laughed: "And who, little friend, were they?"

"The dark, huddled emigrants in the steerage at night," I told him.

"Yes, yes," he replied, "I know. I heard them one night going from Palermo to Naples.... The vessel was new and small, and having examined every detail, we also went to the steerage. There about ten to fifteen Sicilian men sat with their hands folded all in like manner. I thought: 'Do they pray?' And asked a man, but received the sneering answer: 'Do you not see that they are fettered?' Then I noticed the officers in the dim background. Later I heard them sing; it made me think of caged canaries.

"But those officers, the Carabiniere, as the Italian policemen are called, were charming to look at. Their uniform is somewhat antique: a black dress-coat with golden buttons, white leather belt and scabbard, and a Napoleon hat. Very pretty and original.

"When seeing the first Carabiniere I thought there comes at least a general or a minister and didn't know how to salute him. They are a selection of the most handsome men from the army. Italian girls, speaking of their lover, are heard to say: 'He is as handsome as a Carabiniere.'

He said, facing me: "If you were confronted by one on horseback you would think Napoleon had arisen suddenly."

I: "And like you would be at a loss about a proper salute."

He chuckled. "They receive the honors corresponding with their attire," he said. "Most romantic figures. The tales one hears about them exceed those of the well-known Sicilian robbers. They are on everybody's lips and would furnish fine material for an ambitious novelist.... In Italy they have the term: robber-prince. And a princely race they were, who robbed from the rich and gave to the poor. If a peasant's crop failed the bandits helped him out. And because of this understanding with the common people they never were caught. One of them, it is asserted, was the lover of an Italian princess. Whenever his gang visited the city he paid a visit to her.

"They are much like the nobility of today. All nobles were bandits once, whose trade was war, who robbed the peasants if they couldn't pay them tribute.... But then, we are not doing any better today. We have simply given the thing a different name.

"Entering the harbor of Naples," he reflected, "the phrase came to me: Stranger, see Naples and die. It is better to see Naples and live here.

"It is wonderfully situated and resembles Constantinople. But, aside from its fine works of art one finds general uncleanliness. Begging and stealing is practiced among certain classes as a vocation. We ate something in a restaurant and beggars passed constantly among the patrons. They take whatever the customer leaves.

"There are also people whose occupation is to collect cigar-stumps in the city, and there is a booth at the great market where partly smoked cigars are for sale.

"In the old quarter one finds the famous Santa Luggia. A genuine being from there practices the phrase: Sweet inaction. All day long they lie in the sun and wait for what destiny might bring."

"But," I objected, "the song has it otherwise."

"Do you not know that nations as well as individuals usually sing about what they haven't," replied Mr. Ehret with a humorous twinkle. "However, the song may have been true once upon a time. Peter and I too were caught by this sweet inaction, and instead of walking took a cab to see the sights. It is one of the greatest and most inexpensive pleasures in Naples. For a franc you can ride over the whole city, covering about five or six miles.

"The most exciting spectacle we met was a herdsman with his goats in the midst of the city streets. There may have been two or three hundred of them, brown animals with hair as glossy as silk. The herdsman is also the owner and is a capitalist, his goats representing a value of fifteen to twenty thousand lire.

"The Italian thinks much of beautiful shoes and hats. And so this man strides along elegantly dressed from foot to head, a whip in hand. Something very singular; a poetical figure. In a melodious tune he calls through the streets that the goats are here. A door opens here and there. Every goat, who, besides a

modestly jingling bell carries the number of the
leaseholder, runs into the kitchen where they milk
her, then comes out again. Once being led to a certain
house she never makes a mistake.

"The Neapolitan goat milk is the only milk I ever
tasted that smelled nice. Any other kind, especially
that of cows, has a disagreeable odor when boiling.
But then, they always live in the open and feed on
herbs otherwise used for medical purposes. Hence
their milk smells like flowers. Contrary to reputation,
goats are very particular about their food
....Of those herbs the monks make wonderful
healing drinks."

With a broad smile: "I once lived with a German
family near Jerusalem. The German, it is known,
likes milk in his coffee—a custom foreign to the
Oriental. One may have camel's milk, but cows are
not raised there because there is little grass. Now, the
little German colony obtained milk  from neigh-
boring farms. A woman came daily with the bottles.

"One day my landlord overheard the chatter of two
milk women. As everywhere the first question always
is: How is business? His milk woman confided to the
other that she had done well this year. By adding
water to the milk she had made so much that she was
now able to buy her husband another wife, she said.

"The farmer is an idler," Mr. Ehret explained. "The
wife takes all the responsibility and does all the work.
To have relief in the house she buys her husband
another wife instead of hiring help. It is cheaper, and
a more dignified proceeding in their eyes. In spite of

tales to the contrary, the Oriental woman is something holy. If she dies her capital goes not to her husband, as in Europe, but always to her parents—and so does his."

"Then he has no control over her money at all?" I questioned.

"No," said Mr. Ehret, "though sometimes they put what they have together."

"And what is the smallest price for a wife?"

"Five hundred francs.... Every beggar there has to be able to show that much.... Besides, the woman is not veiled because of her husband's lordliness, as a possession which he chooses to hide, but because she is sacred. To stare at a feminine person behind a veil is an offence."

# 23

# The Most Ideal Spot on Earth

Returning to Naples another time and dwelling on the museum and the relics of Herculaneum and Pompeii at the foot of Vesuvius, Mr. Ehret said: "Six thousand years have now passed over it and still one finds paintings so well preserved as if they were made today. All modern paintings pale, but the ancients had a chemistry so wonderful that although they painted on lime their colors kept.

"Above Naples, upon a mount, stands a cloister by the name of Kamaldoli. With surrounding nature: garden, flowers, view, and the soul of the place, its peaceful life, it is the most ideal spot on earth. I sat there in the garden under an arbor trying to picture an isle of the blessed, but could not imagine anything better than this place with its ideal beings and its outlook upon the gulf of Naples.

"Lacremae Christi (tears of Christi) the wine is called which they put before you. It is grown only by those monks, doesn't contain alcohol but puts one in a wonderful mood.

"One day we met a funeral in Naples. It was a strange procession—no corpse was there. That remains at home while the mourners parade through the entire city. What we call pallbearers are about fifteen men clothed in white mantles, wearing white masks. They accompany the hearse, murmuring a continuous funeral prayer, half song and very dismal."

Knowing the old custom in his own country I asked if he didn't sing at funerals as a child. He said yes. "But I would not bring sweetened coffee to the neighbors after the funeral, nor eat the white rolls." Just as if he was still the little boy, priding himself that he simply couldn't be made to do certain things.

"We went to Rome, the holy city," he said again. "While Naples has a strictly southern character where one still sees native beings with a bad reputation but who are not really dangerous, where the streets are dirty and houses crumbling, Rome is the contrary, modern and clean. Instead of Lazeroni, beggar and streetwalker, the main type here is the soldier and the clergyman. Accordingly, the wonderful monumental buildings of classic times are changed into barracks.

"Here, too, the chief sights of the city are its churches, with St. Peter's at the head, and here also one has to bow to the middle ages. There are Greek antiquities, stone blocks fifteen hundred meters high, of which the modern builders say that they could not be placed where they now are by any skill known today.

"St. Peter's is a building of such vastness, beauty and marvelous technical finish. The cupola, owing to its range, is one of the widely acclaimed wonders. According to the reckoning of present technologists it would have to fall any minute, but doesn't. Men like Michelangelo and Bramante have worked on it. Next to the Egyptian pyramids it is the greatest and most artful building ever created by human hands. Two or several choirs may sing in it at the same time without disturbing each other.

"Of the about three hundred churches in Rome one surpasses the other in classic beauty.

"Then there is the residence of the pope, the Vatican, also a structure of beauty, open to visitors. I was surprised to find there not only the greatest works of art, but the best endowed museum, with only marble and gold.

"At that time, when we came to Rome a French president held his entry. Carnot, I presume, was his name. He later was assassinated. During his regency the law was passed that all Catholic brotherhoods were to be banished from France, and so the Vatican wore mourning. The place lay in darkness while the

city was changed into a sea of light. Such
illumination.... I should not care to live in Rome."

"Too pious?" I asked.

He shook his head. "Too much surface. It gives one a
hunger for green fields or even a desert of sand.
However, most cities do that to me.

"We went to Florence, the heart of classic paintings.
It is surpassed by Rome only in artful buildings and
sculpture. Boeklin, the great painter, lived in its
neighborhood.... About twenty or thirty years ago,
from 1880-1900, Italy was still very poor and
squandered its works of art. So a law exists now that
no painting is allowed to leave the country, be the
offer what it may.

"From Florence the road naturally seems to lead one
to Pisa, with its oblique tower of an interesting
church, and then to Genoa. All the way there we had
been journeying more below than above the ground
and arrived as black as chimney sweeps. Beggars
met us at the depot, telling the same old story as
everywhere. One learns to take them for granted in
that country, like its music or its art. I was about
seven or eight times at the station and always was
accosted by the same individuals with the same
complaint.

"Characteristic in Genoa is the so-called gobble
street, where the busy workers eat their dinner. There
everything imaginable is to be had in the line of food,
and the things are served right out of the pan into
one's hand. People eat there standing in the street. By

overhead illumination, amid the cries of everyone offering his things as the best, this is something wonderful.

"The old city lies by the sea; the modern, the residence part of town stretches in marvelous beauty along a mountain slope. Tall buildings, none less than seven or eight stories high, are typical of old Genoa. One of them was topped by a wine arbor. Imagine the strength and length of this grape-vine. Its feet below and its crown up there, and all without modern care. The owner didn't know anything about disinfection and the like, didn't even give it manure. And it bore the finest of grapes. It was an inspiration.

"Being a seaport town, Genoa has a certain colorful life, something free, international. With it ends all that is typical Italian, except its famous cemetery, the Campo Santo, meaning the holy field. It lies near Genoa and is the most beautiful in the whole world. The grounds alone are a work of art. Well-to-do people have a family grove over which they build a chapel. Usually the head or whole figure of the dead hewn in marble is seen as monument, pictured as angel or the life.... There was a time when I regarded this death worship as sacriligeous until a man reminded me that whenever one goes to the cemetery to bring flowers one always brings so much love. And that, of course, means so much health and sanity. Some day hate shall be known for what it is: a disease; *love is mental cleanliness.*

"Another famous cemetery is in Milan, but less beautiful. In a suburb of that city there also remains a painting by Leonardo da Vinci: The Lord's Supper.

But it is in a bad condition, for the French, during one of the Neapolitanic wars, used that building as a stable for their horses."

# 24

# The Isle of Capri

"Capri," Mr. Ehret was saying, "I had wanted to see it all my life, had pictured it as the one blessed isle since our village teacher first mentioned its name. And now we were hardly an hour's distance from there. The official steamer of the English takes one across in that time, charging five lire. For the native, or those who know the custom, the trip is thirty centimes. We paid the thirty cts.

"This island is about eight miles long and six miles wide. Upon it lived until recent years a simple fisher race, untouched by culture, who beside fishing pursued the fruit and wine cultivation. It is of such picturesque beauty, its shores as well as its houses, the inhabitants and their costumes, that the greatest painters and poets of the last centuries conceived their motives there.

"There now my friend and I went with the resolution of taking a final fasting cure. My old complaint had returned and I no longer wanted to live half sick and half well.... It was summer when we arrived, and no season for tourists. That time of the year the island is too hot for them.

"There then was the question of an abode. However, we found a residence in a vineyard, a brand new, furnished house amid grapevines and fig-trees. We rented two rooms but had the whole place at our disposal. It suited us.

"This residence was wonderfully situated, on the southern side with its very steep slope, so steep that one couldn't walk down. On the beautiful strand below was a little inn, and from there a group of rocks projected out into the ocean whereupon sat a number of painters. Until a few years ago that place could be reached only by boat. Then the well-known cannon king, Krupp, built a zigzag stairway down along this face of a rocky precipice.

"He was a frequent visitor at Capri, spending nearly every winter there. The street is called Via Krupp. With his great wealth he easily made himself popular on the island, he and a friend, the well-known German painter Allers, who is famous for his sketches of the chancellor Bismark. But towards the end of the nineties the newspapers began to talk about him and his affairs there, keeping it up for

severn or eight months. Slander, of course. For," he
remarked humorously, "what else could hold the
interest of the public for such a length of time?
However, nobody learned what really was at the
bottom of it all. One fine day the artist Allers had
vanished and their residence was shown to visitors
by a poor man for a tip.

"Here still lay his belongings, the paint-brush his
hand held to the last, etc. It gave me the peculiar
feeling of some one having died by violence and the
loving bereaved ones being loath to disturb his
things. But, there was no foundation to tbis, of
course. Nobody knew what had become of him, and I
do not believe that anybody greatly cared, for apart
from being a known artist the man had remained a
stranger. Only one thing is certain, that had he not
vanished, the Italian government would have sent
him to jail.

"Krupp too had left—for home. Three days later a
telegraph made known to the world that he had died
of heart failure. Naturally, he was buried in all
honors. The Kaiser himself strode along as foremost
mourner behind the coffin. But that was not the end.
The public tongues aren't satisfied to let an event like
that rest. The press is always eager for sensational
stories. And so it brought the strangest and absur-
dest conjectures to light, crying about if for a whole
year.

"Certain it is that Allers had something on the score
and that Krupp participated in it. What the Capri-
cians whispered about looked pretty dark. Krupp had
committed suicide, they said, but that was revoked;

also the statement that the funeral of Krupp in imperial parade was a comedy, that a puppet was buried while he escaped to some foreign country.

"A few weeks after this funeral there appeared in the leading organ of the German social democrat, the Vorwaerts, the following insert: We pay anybody 1000 marks who can prove that it was the dead body of Krupp which lay in that coffin.

"And did they prove it?" I wanted to know.

"No," said Mr. Ehret. "In time the drivelling talk fell asleep. Had things, however, not happened precisely as they did the imperial house, as Krupp's best friend, would have suffered a terrible scandal.... Not even a suicide could have re-established his morality. Italy would have had to deliver him up as a criminal.

"Now, everybody abroad talked about a Villa Krupp and that didn't exist. They mistook it for Via Krupp, the historic street in doubtful light which Peter and I walked daily to catch up from the ocean's sand those glowing beams of the July sun and then take a bath in the deep water. It is so clear that one believes to be looking into the endless when looking down there.

"That sun bath was so hot that it really was a roasting. An Italian passing by regarded us with strange looks. I always thought he wanted something, but he always called: 'For God's sake, cover the head! It is perilous to life to lie thus in the sun.'

"When we could stand the heat no longer we took refuge in a cave nearby, made charming and poetical

because it could not be reached by land. We swam
there."

"The Blue Grotto, that wonderful Stalactite cave
about which one reads so much in novels?" I asked.

"No. That is on the other side of the island,"
explained Mr. Ehret. "Its rocks are white and it has a
waterfall. The water is so blue that its reflex makes
the white rocks appear the same.

"But," he went on to say, "the day had come when I
no longer could trust myself to the water and was now
two hours climbing the street that Peter and I had
formerly climbed in twenty minutes. Both of us were
fasting. Yet, though my body was weak, I often felt
like Odysseus, so that Peter made fun of me, saying
that only the harp was missing.

"Who could help singing of a splendor more beautiful
than all other Italian Poesy because it is an island? It
is the most picturesque place, and never in my life
have I understood the happiness, the beauty of
solitude as well as there. I now knew the why of just
such an island with its people and their achieve-
ments, where every house is a poem. My spirit grew
younger as my body grew weaker. At the same time a
longing took hold of me for those other blessed isles of
which poets have sung from Demethines to
Nietzsche.

"Not only as if the sea in its billows talked, but every
stone and little grass had a language. Of Demethines, that Greek singer, it also is said that he
made his poems in a solitary, rocky cave by the sea.

"While during those hours of spiritual uplift I hardly felt my body, it grew worse, and during the last eight days I couldn't go out any more. Half dead I lay in bed.

"Peter, who had been trying to cure himself of stammering, broke his fast on the ninth day. He was hoarse, and went to buy four pounds of figs from a farmer. 'And how much are they?' he asked. Said the farmer: 'What? How much? Figs do not cost anything. We feed daily from thirty to forty pounds to the pigs. We do not eat any.'

"Peter ate the whole platter full—four pounds at once," said Mr. Ehret with an amused smile. "He grumbled thereby like an animal. When finished his hoarseness was worse. But in two more days not only his hoarseness was gone but also the stammer.

"I myself fasted for twenty-three days, feeling miserable towards the end. I couldn't sleep, but tossing about on my pillow at night I always dreamt of Odysseus and the blessed isles.

"The result of this fast was much better than in Algiers. Again we began to wander. Going back to Naples we made a journey on foot through the whole of Southern Italy."

He concluded, wistfully: "Life is the same everywhere, the same problems, joy, grief, success, failure. We are all actors playing our given part; the clothes, the scenery may differ; underneath we are alike. Having seen and understood one phase of life one has seen all."

# 25

# The Isle of Life, Land of the Blessed

When finished I asked if all this happened before he went to Askona. He said: "Yes. Before I ever heard of it."

I: "Then there your search for that blessed isle ended? You found it in Capri?"

He shook his head. "I am still looking for it."

"But what do you think it should be like?"

"What do I think it should be like?" he repeated slowly after me. Then: "I had a dream one night, or rather a series of dreams, telling it better than I could.... Previous to that I had been thinking about my second rebirth at Capri and how perfect it was due to the spiritual regeneration preceding it. I began to see how little the material part of me really had counted, how spirit alone had done the good work, spirit and water and sun. And I understood that this could have been possible only in the solitude of an island, away from people in their crowded dwellings, as had been the case with Christ in the wilderness and the hermit in the woods.

"So I dreamt about an isle of life, the undiscovered land of the blessed. And this was it:

"My friend and I wandered away, through many countries and across far oceans, apart from the crowds of people. Our feet were as light as the stag's. And glad, and ever more ardent became our mood. The forest was our house, soft moss the bed. We aimed further towards the sun and were led into the sphere of eternal summer. The beams of the heavenly constellation showed us the way to the blessed isle where in undamaged forests gentle animals dwelt, where paradisical food ripens between glowing stones and uncultivated earth.

"Then again it seemed as if for days at a time we wandered through a forsaken valley, which I should name Black Valley, because nothing but blackberries grew there. Now, the more seldom we saw water the more abundant we found wild fruits. We never talked now; nature had so much to say. Even the stones seemed to converse. And a stillness vibrated about it all whose invisible beauty we could feel. It was something like an all-surrounding, holy soul with whom one may exchange words or thoughts, had not its very presence made words and thoughts unnecessary.

"At another time Zarathustra spoke to our hearts, saying: 'There are still thousands of life's islands, thousands of ways that never were walked; undiscovered still is man and man's earth.' So we glided on: we were so light that our feet didn't touch the ground.

"And then all at once we saw the blessed isle lie there in the rosy east, on the warm, glorious waters. Navigators had never stirred across those seas. They would have been pulled down into the depth by its impelling whirls. For there the flaming sun had its birth and whatever came close to that fiery ball must die.

"Evidently we had passed the border of all life. Our own flame of being was not from the slow fire of mankind. But when we would pass darkness came upon us, and instead of the bright island there was a black colossus resting upon the sea like a giant ship with masts and smoke stacks.

"Presently we noticed huge shadows of rocks, cypresses and other tall, strange trees, and then we saw the rocks grow white and a silvery light fall upon the water, shining down into its very bottom. A picture of creation. The bright light had only clothed itself in darkness that we may witness its birth.

"Like an infant it lay there in the purple glory of the morning. Birds, as white and gentle as doves, as large as eagles, encircled its steep shores and the tree tops. Swans with graceful necks crossed like watchmen before the isle as before a sanctuary. A cave gaped with its deep gulf against the continent as though it were the door to the dwelling of the blessed.

"Having had before the feeling of unearthly lightness of body we now crossed easily. By the entrance of the cave the great secret dawned upon us that we had passed through the baptism of fire, the fire of the holy ghost, else we could never have reached that country, that sea, that island. It was sheltered from all beings not purified by a life of mental cleanliness, stripped of every material longing. Those living there had burned all dross in their being. In the glowing light of the Highest they had transformed themselves into spirit.

"We now heard the heavenly voices of the blest. A glorious being startled us. It was a womanly figure surrounded by ethereal light. As she came near all the voices were heard singing: Love is the fulfilling of the law.

"The shining one was Hilda. I recognized her by that first look whose undying power had united us so long ago.... My friend, who never had loved the pure soul of a woman, threw himself sobbing at her feet, covering his head before her glory. Then we went back to earth to fulfill that great law for which alone man was destined to live."

I had nothing to say and Mr. Ehret looked up with his old smile and said goodbye. I was bound for a northern journey; he went to Los Angeles.

The End.

# Appendix

## Editor's Note

The following Appendix contains Arnold Ehret's basic theory of his Mucusless Diet Healing System.

Lecturing in Europe and America he provided his audiences with the "Master Key". It is just as effective today as it was decades ago. Always appealing in its natural simplicity, now even more convincing. His system has withstood the test of time—the ultimate test of truth. We need to be guided by this gentle man's prophetic words. The increasing tempo of modern life and its assault on our well-being, demands that we become self-reliant in matters concerning our personal health and happiness.

We're pleased to announce the publication of Arnold Ehret's personal primer on the practical self-application of fasting and the Mucusless Diet Healing System. Dedicated to Dr. Benedict Lust over 50 years ago by Ehret, it has been withheld from publication by their mutual agreement to allow the test of time to prove its validity.

*"Maximum benefit can be derived from a fasting cure or a mucusless diet undertaken for the purpose of rejuvenation or as a diet healing system, if the following rules are observed."* are Ehret's welcome opening words to thousands of us who have needed and waited for his book, INSTRUCTIONS FOR FASTING AND DIETING.

For your copy, please order directly from:

BENEDICT LUST LIBRARY
P.O. Box 404 * Murray Hill
New York, NY 10156

Price: $2.95 + 75¢ for handling.

Also available from your favorite Book Store or Health Food Shop.

# Building Bodily Health, Strength and Efficiency

## Arnold Ehret's Basic Lecture

During my early Twenties I first became severely sick with Bright's disease. I was on the verge of the grave, after being told by orthodox medical physicians that my illness was incurable. Responding to an "inner call", I fought my way to absolute health; a state of health that remains today, far better than when I did my military service. I found relief through different methods of nature-cure and drugless healing as practiced at that time. It became necessary for me to include Nature's infallible remedies—the only methods that can truly overcome disease—they are: fasting and an exclusive fruit diet.

Neither of these factors were given consideration nor credit for their potential healing qualities by any of the various healing arts. In fact, even today, acknowledgment still continues to be sorely lacking—both by medical science and the average layman interested in his own health regime. It took years of study, testing and self-experimentation, which often bordered upon the dangerous, before I finally came upon the truth. The truth is, no matter what you may be suffering from, regardless of how feverish, weak or desperately ill you may feel, *Nature wants to save you*. Disease is merely Nature's effort to start the process of healing—the elimination of waste and disease matters that clog up your cellular system. Listen to the instinctive advice of Nature given to both man and animals. "Give me a chance to eliminate; to repair your bodily mechanism. Take time to be sick for a few days or even weeks, and I'll help you. Remain still, quiet, rest, sleep and *don't eat.*"

When you obstruct Nature's good intentions through the use of man-made synthetic drugs—or continue eating more and more of the disease producing foods—or if the quantities of waste, mucus and poisons in your body are too much and too old—or too many of your vital organs have been surgically crippled and the spark of life grows dim—it may be too late.

The selection and preparation of various foods, become immensely important factors of life when you recognize a large percentage of all mankind could not endure a long fast. You can learn more about these surprising facts in my book, the "MUCUSLESS DIET HEALING SYSTEM".* Without a corrective diet perfect health cannot be attained through modern miracle drugs or any form of "orthodox" medicine or through mechanical treatments. A supreme, absolute, Paradisical health—the way of infallible healing must be achieved through, and is ruled by, the laws of diet. Man, like every living plant and organism matures and owes his existence to food. Man's health or his disease of every description result directly from food intake. His state of mind may be a contributing factor, but the fall of mankind in the final analysis is "sin of diet". The real

*Mucusless Diet Healing System* by Arnold Ehret.
Benedict Lust Publications, P.O. Box 404,
New York, NY 10156.
$2.25 + 75¢, handling costs.

physiological cause of the physical ailments of
mankind can be traced directly to the present-day
accepted diet of civilization. Having allowed your
body to degenerate through over eating wrong,
disease producing food, prayer alone will prove
unavailing without a physical effort being made to
correct your wrong living habits. Mankind's return to
the ideal prototype of the "perfect" normal being will
require a complete healing from the sins of the diet of
civilization as practiced today. Disease is internal
uncleanliness acquired over all ages by wrong foods.
My revelation of disease and their healing through
corrective diet is based on proof and backed by
experience and experiments conducted on my own
body as well as on thousands of patients at Dr.
Benedict Lust's *YUNGBORN SANITARIUM* during
a period of over five years. All methods of natural
treatments are indeed more or less cleansing, healing, regenerating and rejuvenating, but fail to completely overcome the cause—which is the direct effect
of the "clogging-up" process. A well selected cleansing diet consisting of fresh fruits and green leaf
vegetables make it a pleasure rather than a painful
experience. The choice of food making many varia-
tions possible, the prescribed rest and relaxation are
indicated in each case and must be especially selected
to meet the individual needs. For example, careful
determination of the quantity of waste and poisons in
the daily elimination of mucus being dissolved and
carried off by the blood stream, should be recognized.
The coated tongue and sample specimen of urine,
putrid fecal matter are all tell-tale evidence. The vital
efficiency of the patent should not obstructed,
therefore a slowing-down of the aggressive effect of

elimination is advisable. The more time allowed for
the body to throw off accumulated poisons, the less
vitality will be required to do the work, and the more
certain successful results. For example: when a case
history shows that drugs have been used over a long
period of time, it becomes extremely advisable to slow
down the aggressive effect of elimination through the
use of cooked foods—especially vegetables contain-
ing roughage,—such as is found in beets, beet tops,
spinach, celery, etc. If the ailment is at all curable,
Nature heals not only the disease, but the whole man.
It may require as long as one to three years of
systematically continued natural cleansing diets
and fasting for the average "well" person before the
body is cleansed of toxic matters. Assuring results
will of course be noticed within the first few weeks.
You may then see how the body is constantly
eliminating waste by way of the urinary canal, the
colon, eyes, ears, nose and throat; via every pore of
your skin over the entire surface of your body. You
will observe how both "wet" and "dried" mucus,
(dandruff, scaly formations in the nose, wax in the
ear drums, for instance) is being continuously
expelled. You will agree with me when I state that all
diseases of mankind, both mental and physical have
the same foundational cause—whatever the symp-
toms may be. It is without a single exception one and
the same universal condition; a unity of disease;
waste, foreign matter, excess mucus, and their
related poisons. For example, offensive odor or
"invisible waste". Everyone, no matter to what
extent he may claim to enjoy good health has a latent
sickness. A severe shock such as a cold or influenza
starts elimination throughout the entire body. This

attempted house-cleaning by Nature should not be interfered with, either by continued eating or the use of drug suppressants. Nature should be permitted to eliminate the excess waste, often stored in the body since early childhood. Interference often results in producing acute and chronic diseases. The process of elimination is not a pleasant experience, but how self-satisfying it is to know you have averted a more severe stage of illness a postponement would have eventually made necessary. Man's mastery of disease will bring humanity closer to a perfect human body. If you hope to achieve good health, freedom from pain and illness, and the full enjoyment of Paradisical existence, it can be obtained through proper observance of Nature's laws, inherent in the creation of man himself.

No one needs to live with disease—and freedom from disease has now become a reality. My "Mucusless Diet Healing System" has brought to all who would listen and follow, the information needed to banish illness and suffering. Cleansing is basic for the correction and elimination of disorders caused by the accumulation of poisons and congestion throughout the entire body. Unusable and accumulated waste stored in the tissues cause degeneration and decay. When you stop feeding and start cleansing your system, you allow your body to return to normalcy. Magic cures, witchcraft or miracle drugs cannot possibly eliminate the cause of any disease. The cleansing diet is at the same time a body building diet—leaving the body free from the accumulation of toxic waste brought about by eating "mucus-forming" foods. Skin disorders and other conditions such

as boils, abscesses, and carbuncles are Nature's
unceasing effort to eliminate excess waste. Poisons
will disappear quickly from the body. Correct foods,
(fruits and green leaf vegetables) allow Nature to
build a strong, healthy body; wrong foods produce a
diseased body. We can eliminate all suffering,
ailments and disease through the physiological
operations of diet. Foods, manufactured by man, only
cause disease, troubles and sickness, and are therefore wrong foods. Right foods, fresh fruits and
green-leaf vegetables are healthy, divine foods,
healing and diseaseless; Paradisical living. Believ-
ing, knowing, having complete faith in these truthful
facts and their scientific application, is the infallible
principle of all healing, the real knowledge that must
eventually result in the physiological salvation of
mankind. In our society today man gets too much
food—not too little. We must realize the limitations of
the human digestive system.

Disease is Nature's effort to rid the body of disease
matters and eliminate waste from the system. The
deeper causes of internal uncleanliness and its
resulting constipation, can be definitely corrected
and overcome through my teachings, not merely
relieved. This has proven to be the one true, practical,
and scientific road to regeneration. The simplicity
and naturalness of my method appeals to the
intelligent person interested in self-betterment of
body, mind and soul.

The complete works of Arnold Ehret, including newly released manuscripts, are now available directly from the publisher in paperback editions.

Orders for the complete set will receive a **FREE SAMPLE** of the new **ARNOLD EHRET POSTER**.

For latest Book List and Order Blank, write to the publisher:

**BENEDICT LUST PUBLICATIONS**
P. O. Box 404
New York, NY 10156

For Complete Catalog
of Natural Health Literature
send 25¢ to

**BENEDICT LUST PUBLICATIONS**

The Original Health Book People

**P.O. Box 404
New York, NY 10156**